THE
WANDERING
COMPANY

Ismail Merchant

J. F. Ivory

R. Prawer Jhabvala

TWENTY-ONE YEARS
OF MERCHANT IVORY FILMS

Ismail Merchant, Ruth Prawer Jhabvala, James Ivory

THE WANDERING COMPANY

TWENTY-ONE YEARS OF MERCHANT IVORY FILMS

by

JOHN PYM

Comments by James Ivory

BFI PUBLISHING

British Film Institute, London/The Museum of Modern Art, New York

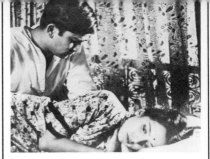

Twenty-one years of Merchant
Ivory Productions: 'The
Householder' (left strip) and
'The Courtesans of Bombay'
(right)

In Memory
MATTHEW JOHN HOARE

Designed by Edwin Taylor

Published by the British Film Institute
127 Charing Cross Road
London WC2H 0EA
and the Museum of Modern Art
W 53rd Street, New York
N.Y. 10019

British Library Cataloguing in Publication Data
Pym, John
The wandering company: twenty-one years of
Merchant Ivory films
1. Ivory – James
1. Title
791.43'0233'0924   PN1998.A31/

ISBN 0-85170-127-2 BFI
0-87070-630-6 MOMA

Typeset by Face Ronchetti Limited
Printed in Great Britain by
Garden House Press, London NW10

CONTENTS

'The Europeans'

'Heat and Dust'

Jean Renoir's 'The River'

Chapter One

THREE CULTURES

In December 1961, James Ivory, a prospective feature film director, and Ismail Merchant, a prospective feature film producer, travelled by train from Bombay to Delhi and presented themselves with a proposition at the home of Ruth Prawer Jhabvala, the novelist and short-story writer. She had been guarded during a preliminary telephone conversation, Merchant said, pretending at first to be her mother-in-law. The men had come to India from the United States in hopes of making a film about life in a Gujerat village. This project, however, which had originated in New York, had fallen apart through disagreements over the script and because production money failed to materialise in India. Merchant and Ivory were now searching for a new script. They had recently decided to form a production company and were looking for a film with which to launch it. Some time earlier, in Los Angeles, Merchant had read and been impressed by Ruth Jhabvala's novel *The Householder*. The studios would never consider turning it into a film, he had been told by an experienced Hollywood scriptwriter, Isobel Lennart, but it would make an excellent property for an as yet untried independent outfit. In Delhi, Merchant and Ivory prevailed upon Ruth Jhabvala to adapt her modest novel about the trials marriage sets two young Indians.* [An asterisk in the text denotes a marginal note by James Ivory.] A script was written within a few weeks, and shortly afterwards filming of *The Householder* began under the banner of Merchant Ivory Productions.

Twenty-one years later, Merchant Ivory Productions has completed a total of eighteen feature, short and documentary films. The company has travelled the world. It has used locations in, among other places, Delhi, Bombay, Benares, Hyderabad, London, Oxford, Paris, New York, California, New Hampshire and Massachusetts. The company still lives out of a suitcase, improvises its offices, relies on friends. It remains an independent outfit, exists on its wits. 'Nothing has become easier,' Merchant says. 'With each new film the stakes are raised, we have to risk more. That's part of the game.'

JI: Thus began our collaboration. But not without some apprehension on both sides. On our side because we had been led to believe that Ruth – she then used the cryptic initial 'R' instead of her given name – was difficult to approach, to know, was almost a recluse, living a highly private life behind the walls of her compound in Old Delhi, seeing no one. And on her side as well, having already been approached by stage and film producers, who then evaporated without explanation. She would have been even more uneasy if she had known that the main members of the abandoned Gujerat film were being promised starring parts by Ismail in *The Householder*. As it turned out, the players, Shashi Kapoor, Leela Naidu and Durga Khote, adapted perfectly to the new story. A bigger piece of legerdemain was to hold on to the same investors for two utterly different films, but Ismail managed to do that, too.

THE PRODUCER

Ismail Merchant was born in Bombay on 25 December 1936 into a family, on his father's side, of traders and business people. In hopes of a son, his mother, who had already given birth to three daughters, tied a ribbon to the gate of the shrine of her particular saint, Khawja Moinuddin Chistie, at Ajmer in Rajasthan. Three more girls were born after Ismail. During the 1940s, Merchant's father, who dealt chiefly in textiles, though he later had interests in motorcars and racehorses, prospered. Merchant recalls the pleasure which he and his sisters experienced when their father came home with his pockets full of money, his winnings at the track.

One of Merchant's earliest memories is of the family grouped round the radio listening to the war news. Although events in Europe seemed distant, Merchant's childhood was impressed by local Indian politics. His father, the devout president of a Bombay branch of the Muslim League, was well regarded by his Hindu neighbours; but both he and they suffered in the city riots which preceded Partition in 1947. 'I still have nightmares about those riots,' Merchant said. 'Our politics then centred on the feeling that, simply, the British must leave. My friends and I drove about in lorries waving banners. We grew up on slogans.' Although many relatives did emigrate to Pakistan, Merchant's father held to his determination that he and his family should remain in India.

A boyhood incident which Merchant judges of great moment and which, he believes, fundamentally shaped his attitude to his future career as a film producer, occurred in 1945 when, through his father's position, he was charged with learning a long religious speech spiked with political references to Partition. Merchant was coached by a mullah and the speech was delivered to acclaim before a crowd of 10,000 Sunni Moslems in Bombay at the culmination of the ten-day observances of the Moslem New Year, Muharram. 'I was aware then that I could speak to people and somehow make them believe in me,' Merchant said. 'Although I don't think I understood then what I was really saying – the political undertones – I did understand that I had stirred up that crowd, and that there was no way in which I could calm it down. Now, once one of our films starts, it is like that crowd, there is no going back, no stopping. I knew I could move the crowd and I know I can finish the film. This is the attitude I have always adopted.'

In 1949, a young woman, Nimmi, a film actress at the start of her career, paid a call on the Merchant household. Her family was from Agra, she knew few people in Bombay. She took to Ismail, who had a gift for friendship and seemed unabashed by the difference in their ages. Her first film, *Barsaat*, directed by

Ismail Merchant, Susan Hayward

Raj Kapoor (the family name will recur later in this story), was a success. Merchant, meanwhile, was growing up on a diet of Hollywood movies. What more could one ask than to be friends with a star? 'She would arrive at our house in a convertible Cadillac and the crowds would gather, and then she would take me to the studios (there were then some 25 in Bombay) and say "You must become a star".' Later, returning from a trip to England, where she had met Alexander Korda, Nimmi showed Merchant her souvenir photographs: he insisted, having already produced several successful school entertainments, that they were going to make films together in America. (He was as good as his word in that in Merchant Ivory Productions' first feature, *The Householder*, there is a tribute to Nimmi. The hero of the film, Prem, beset by the responsibilities of marriage, dreams of carefree days when he had the time and money to go to the cinema. He remembers Nimmi and we see an excerpt from her film *Daag* [1952].)

By the time he was admitted to St Xavier's College, Bombay, in 1954, having attended both Jesuit and Moslem secondary schools, Merchant had fixed his mind on the cinema and show business. He had no enthusiasm for his father's wish that he become a barrister or a doctor. 'I would wait for hours outside Nimmi's house until she returned from shooting. Even when her films failed at the box office, I used to fight for her. Some people said dismissively, "Oh, she's a film star, a commoner." ' (She came from the songstress class to which, in 1982, Merchant paid tribute in his film *The Courtesans of Bombay*.) 'I said, "To hell with it, I'm not interested in *respectability*, I'm interested in who I like." I was very one-track minded. By now I had been introduced to other stars, like Nargis, but none was as friendly as Nimmi.'

Merchant's time at Xavier's, from which he graduated in 1958 with an Arts BA, was marked by his zeal for showmanship. 'Previously the college quadrangle had only been used for religious services and College Day,' Merchant said. 'I argued with conviction, the Jesuit principal surrendered with resigned good humour, and my variety shows were mounted in the quad.' Merchant also acted in college productions, his first role, improbably, being one of the Wise Men in a Nativity play. In his second year, he made up his mind to go to the United States where he intended to produce films with mixed Indian and Hollywood casts. *Samson and Delilah*, *I'll Cry Tomorrow*, *Gone With the Wind*, *Three Coins in the Fountain*, *Roman Holiday*, *The Wizard of Oz*, *Rear Window*, *Dial M for Murder*, *Love is a Many-Splendored Thing* were among the films which cemented this determination. 'I was, of course, also impressed in my early days by Indian films,' Merchant said, 'particularly those of producer-directors like Mehboob Khan and Raj Kapoor. The stars played a crucial role in these films – Nargis, Dilip Kumar, Suraiya, Raj Kapoor, Noor Jehan, Nimmi. I was fascinated going to premieres and watching the mobs: it thrilled me. Films like *Andaz*, *Aag*, *Barsaat*, *Jugnu*, *Dastan* I saw six or seven times. If a film of my favourite star did not succeed at the box office, it upset me. I waited impatiently for the arrival of their new films, announced by huge cinema hoardings, their luridly painted faces looking down. This was the capital of Indian films and I lived right in the heart of it all.'

Merchant was accepted for an MA course in business administration at New York University, but these were lean days for his father and, to raise money for his passage to the United States, Merchant was compelled to mount one more variety show. He had meantime made the acquaintance of several well-regarded musicians and composers, and the immensely popular team of Shankar Jaikishan (who were later employed as composers on MIP's *Bombay Talkie*) were invited as chief guests. This ploy for attracting a large star-gazing audience, who paid handsomely, had already worked when Nimmi was his guest. It may be noted that the regal presence of a star in the audience was incorporated in MIP's second feature, *Shakespeare Wallah* where, however, the effect was somewhat different: a jealous Bombay film star (Madhur Jaffrey) places herself in a box at the rear of the stalls during a live performance of *Othello*; she makes a discreet autograph-signing commotion, all eyes turn from the stage and her rival in love, the actress playing Desdemona (Felicity Kendal), boils inwardly.

'Dial M for Murder'

'The principles of my working life were founded early,' Merchant said. 'I made friends with the people whom I wanted to work for me. They believed in me, I created a sort of confidence in them. I spent generously on them. I took them to Chinese restaurants and paid the bill. I invited them home. As a young man, I did not cook, but my mother prepared wonderful feasts for my friends.' In New York, Merchant held to his principles and quickly made a score of friends, including the Indian players Madhur and Saeed Jaffrey, then with the Actors Studio, who were subsequently to be among the most faithful of MIP's extended family of cast and crew members. The city, which made an immediate and vivid impression, seemed to confirm Merchant's belief that for him 'things just happen' and his faith, when they don't, in his ability to make them happen. Employed as a messenger at the United Nations (and also as a city tour guide, though he hardly knew the city), he posed, he said, as a 'diplomat' and took to entertaining his friends in the delegates' lounge. He was later interviewed for a better-paid job at the advertising agency McCann Erickson: a judicious UNICEF Christmas card, illustrated with an Indian motif, was sent to the man in personnel, and Merchant was hired.

New York introduced Merchant to European cinema and to Satyajit Ray's *Pather Panchali* (1955) and *Aparajito* (1956). In India, he had read about *Pather Panchali*'s 1956 Cannes festival prize, but, in Bombay, he had never had the opportunity to see the Bengali director's work. 'It changed my opinion of all those Hollywood films,' he said. 'Snap, like that. Suddenly it was Ray, Bergman, De Sica, Fellini, I went avidly to *their* films. I continued to go to

Hollywood films, but these European films became a passion. De Sica affected me greatly. I loved Bergman's *Smiles of a Summer Night*? This was the kind of film Merchant now wished to make. New York, he said, also taught him another valuable lesson. 'If you say something with enough authority, people will accept it, even though it may be contrary to what they feel.' Merchant once appeared on the live TV show *What's My Line?* and convinced the audience, so he said, that he – and not his fellow-guest, the Maharaja of Darbanga – was in fact the bona fide Maharaja. (As Ivory recalled it, however, the real Maharaja got more votes.)

Sensing that he had the means, in the facilities of a prosperous New York advertising agency, Merchant determined to make a short film, *The Creation of Woman*. [Credits for this film and James Ivory's first three films are listed at the end of this chapter.] The creator in this Indian mythological story was the god Brahma. Merchant proposed to take the part himself with Madhur Jaffrey as his creation. However, Charles Schwep, who advanced the minimal $6,000 budget, wanted a more professional film. Three dancers were hired headed by the celebrated Bhaskar Roy Chaudhuri, then the leading exponent of Indian dance in New York. Bhaskar was something of a showman and incorporated in the film, which he choreographed, his celebrated and athletic Dance of Shiva. Charles Schwep directed, Merchant was the executive producer, and Jim McIntyre, from the agency's television department, was the art director.

After graduating from NYU, where he had been studying at night without great enthusiasm, Merchant set off for Los Angeles with his completed 14-minute film and, he said, a thick folder of press cuttings about himself (generated by himself) in the advertising and cinema trade journals. A press release preceded him announcing the arrival of a Mogul producer: he visualised a royal welcome. He had, as ever, schemes to use his New York acting acquaintances in Hollywood-produced Indian pictures. 'All along I had discovered that you didn't need money to achieve something. I had done nothing, but I was confident that I *would* do all the things that I said I had done. I was only worried that when I stepped out of my train in California, there would be a crowd of newspapermen.' 'Alas,' James Ivory said, 'there was no one – or fortunately...'

As matters fell, Merchant found himself working part-time at a clothing store in Westwood and on the 9 p.m. to 4 a.m. shift in the classified ads department of the *Los Angeles Times*. This still left time for the pursuit of contacts and more contacts. He went to the University of California to enquire about enrolling in film courses. 'But I was told I was a producer,' Merchant said. 'I didn't need lessons. Wouldn't I prefer to lecture on Indian film-making?' He visited the studios. A film was planned with Agnes Moorehead in India, another with Susan Hayward. 'At that time,' he said, 'India was considered an exotic place. To be an Indian then – me in my

Ismail Merchant, Agnes Moorehead

17

Jodhpur suit – was something out of the ordinary.'

Meanwhile the Academy of Motion Picture Arts and Sciences informed Merchant that *The Creation of Woman* could not be entered in 1961 for an Academy Award since it had not played the statutory three days in that calendar year in a commercial theatre. Merchant promptly approached the owner of the Fine Arts Cinema in Los Angeles, suggested that his short would make an excellent companion piece to Bergman's *The Devil's Eye* and without more ado secured his three days. *The Creation of Woman* was nominated. Merchant, who had spent nearly a year on the West Coast, then placed an advertisement in the trade press: he was returning to India to make ready for a film, as yet unwritten, but titled *Destiny of Life*, on the subject of reincarnation. Agnes Moorehead and Merchant's new friend Ernest Castaldo, who was subsequently to be used in *The Householder*, as a spiritual Westerner, were to star. (A relic of *Destiny of Life* – the first day's shooting, which was marked, as in India, with a Mohurut celebration and the ritual garlanding of the camera by a pandit – is preserved in *Bombay Talkie*. The guru's home movies of his time in California are in fact Merchant's record of this film that never was.)

Merchant set off for Cannes, where *The Creation of Woman* was screened in competition and where he was encouraged by *Variety*'s Gene Moskowitz. En route, however, he stopped in New York. He was invited to a screening of *The Sword and the Flute*, a short documentary on Indian miniature paintings. The narrator was Saeed Jaffrey, who had also narrated *The Creation of Woman*. Merchant was introduced to the director, James Ivory. 'Conversation flowed,' Merchant said. ('Not quite,' Ivory says. 'He kept popping up to telephone important people.') Merchant was struck by Ivory's empathy for India and things Indian: he had not encountered this before in an American. They discussed Ray's films and listened to records of the Pakistani musicians Nazakat and Salamat Ali, and Merchant agreed to help Ivory find finance for a film, which Ivory had agreed to photograph,* to be directed by Sidney Meyers from a script by the anthropologist Gittel Steed. In May 1961 the decision was taken to found an Indo-American production company to make English language films in India aimed at the international market.

THE DIRECTOR

James Ivory was born in Berkeley, California, on 7 June 1928. His paternal grandfather had emigrated to the United States from Ireland in the 1870s; and his father, who had been raised in upstate New York, had come West to further a career on the management side of the lumber business. Ivory's father, who had studied forestry at Syracuse University, entered the business at a time when it was beginning to be treated as a science, when replanting was

JI: It was more that I persuaded Gittel Steed and Sidney Meyers to agree to my photographing their film, which was to be called *Devgar*. Meyers was dubious, with good reason. I had never shot a feature, never lit an actor or an interior, could never have functioned professionally as a cameraman, despite the colour documentary work I'd done in 16mm. This was more than audacious self-confidence, which I realised at once as soon as Subrata Mitra got to work on *The Householder*.

beginning to replace the wholesale felling of woodlands and forests. His mother, who came from an old Louisiana family of mixed French and English ancestry, had met his father when she was sixteen. They had corresponded during the First World War, when he had served in France, and were married soon after.

Although Ivory's mother was a freethinker, and had been brought up unconstrained by the religious if not the political orthodoxies of the South, his son – as was the custom in 'mixed marriages' – was raised in his father's religion, Roman Catholicism. 'I was taught by nuns at a parochial school until I was 13,' Ivory said, 'but I wouldn't say I had a religious upbringing. I had a somewhat theatrically devout period in seventh grade, for a few months, but that is the only time I can remember.'

As a boy, Ivory had his own theatre, built by his father, with a big unadorned roll-up canvas curtain. 'There wasn't really much in the way of sets,' he said, 'and we didn't really do much in the way of plays, but it was a theatre.' His father encouraged him. Ivory's consuming interests were Ancient Egypt, the *ancien régime*, the 'winning of the West' and plantation life in the South. 'One of my favourite film images when I was growing up was of a Yankee officer, cigar at a rakish angle, setting fire to the lace curtains of a plantation house with a candelabra. This was how Hollywood put ante-bellum mansions to the torch. Afterwards the candelabra might be dashed contemptuously through a window pane – as in *Belle Starr*.'

The family, which included a daughter, Charlotte, later moved to the small town of Klamath Falls in southern Oregon not far from which Ivory's father, in partnership with a businessman who had survived the Depression with cash in hand, reactivated a lumber mill, calling it the Ivory Pine Company. As a boy Ivory had been fascinated by buildings, European and American, and by decor. 'If you grew up in a raw Western town, as I did, in a place that has no buildings, except very peculiar ones (the Ford car showroom, for instance, was modelled on the Temple of Karnak, with plate-glass windows in the slanting walls), maybe you just develop a longing for something different or better. Your eye is forever searching the bare landscape for something more solid.'

Ivory was a faithful moviegoer. '*Gone With the Wind*,' he said, 'held me spellbound and I was old enough when it came out in 1939 to appreciate that it was something more than the usual. The Sisters advised us against seeing the film because of its "immorality", but that if we insisted we should clap our hands over our ears when Rhett Butler uttered his profanity.' Other films from boyhood that remain fixed in Ivory's mind include *Marie Antoinette*, *The Swiss Family Robinson*, *Drums Along the Mohawk*, *The Wizard of Oz*, *The Great Waltz*, *Fantasia*, *The Mummy's Hand*, *The Prince and the Pauper*, *Northwest Passage*, *Brigham Young*, *Juarez* and *San Francisco*.*

'My first film,' Ivory said, 'was *Tess of the Storm Country* with Janet Gaynor, in

James Ivory, June 1954

JI: Especially *San Francisco*. When it was re-released in the late 1940s, I hurried to see it. My room at college was next to the little local theatre and I could hear the film through the common wall we shared. (In the same theatre at about the same time I saw my first European 'art' films, wonderful films like *Henry V*, *Day of Wrath* and *Devil in the Flesh*.) When I knew the earthquake sequence was about to begin, because of the rousing musical number that precedes it, I would run around to the box office and wheedle my way in on some pretext, stand in the back and watch San Francisco tumble down, and then come out again. I was always crazy about disaster movies: typhoons and tidal waves and ship-wrecks.

**'The World of Apu' (top),
'Pather Panchali'**

the summer of 1933. There was also a newsreel, a revolution or war in some Latin country, maybe Spain. People rioted in the streets and others dumped objects over a balcony on the crowd below. I remember a full-length statue of a woman being tipped over. It had a form a bit like an Oscar. I remember the newsreel but not the main feature: it is my first memory of seeing a film. I saw dozens and dozens of Westerns by the time I reached my teens – probably a hundred or more – and liked the kindly and urbane Hopalong Cassidy. But as I was growing up in a real Western town, where cowboys and Indians could be seen on the streets and where there were still occasional bar-room shoot-outs, cowboy movies, with their lonesome cabins and dusty, God-forsaken shanty-town streets, didn't hold much appeal for me. Nor did I much like costume films based on literary classics. I preferred them to be based on bestselling, trashier books. When I got to high school, I ate up Bette Davis movies. *Mr Skeffington* was a favourite.'

Ivory's father sold lumber to Metro-Goldwyn-Mayer, and on several occasions, thanks to his father's partner Gus Luellewitz, Ivory was taken on to the studio's working sound stages. 'Like anyone else who watches films being made, this at first appeared to me a very tedious process, if an exacting one. On one occasion, we stood in a large room and were told to keep still. A bell rang, a scene with Ginny Simms in it appeared on a screen, and four men slid on their knees, which were protected by layers of sacking, across the waxed hardwood floor. They did this repeatedly until a voice said "OK" over an intercom. I know now that this was a footsteps session, but it wasn't much to tell the kids about back home. This was 1943.'

Ivory had decided, aged about 14, that he was going to have a career in films as a set designer. At 18, he was admitted to the University of Oregon in Eugene where he studied architecture, but switched in his third year to a general Fine Arts course and as a result took an extra year to graduate. In the summer of 1950, the year before he graduated, Ivory had been to France, with the intention of learning French and enrolling at the IDHEC, the Paris film school. However, the Korean War broke out and to avoid the draft – which, Ivory said, he and other college-educated young Americans fervently wished to avoid – he returned to the United States and enrolled in a graduate programme in film at the University of Southern California. 'Somewhere along in there,' he said, 'I stopped wanting to be a set designer, or *only* a set designer. I knew nothing technical and I failed the entrance exam. But as it was a private school, they were keen to have students – and they took me anyway.' USC did not, however, suit him. 'The teaching was pedestrian. We were almost never given film and a camera, so we rarely had the chance to go out and shoot anything. We were not exactly encouraged to work on films of our own. There had been a scandal: some students had enterprisingly made a pornographic film with the school camera and film stock, and had been caught. This threw a miasma of distrust over our little efforts.

'They were interested in training people who would then go on to make industrial films, and contribute towards what was called "audio-visual education". They didn't prepare people for a career in fiction films. Lip-service was paid, but so little that all the time I was at USC and with all those thousands of dollars of the GI Bill I was never once taken to a studio. That seems incredible, because in 1951, even though television had arrived in a big way, all the studios were still going full-blast and many famous directors and writers were doing their best work, and many famous old-time actors were still very much around. Almost no distinguished professionals from the Hollywood studios came to lecture at the USC Cinema Department. In my two years there, I think only William Cameron Menzies.'

Ivory's first film, *Venice: Theme and Variations*, was made as an MA 'thesis' (in the end, to his annoyance, he had to write the thesis as well, explaining, in thesis language, how he made the film). His father advanced him in all about $15,000, and Ivory set off at the end of 1952, by himself, with a 16mm Bolex camera, a doubtful tripod and a suitcase of film, to shoot 'a history of the city told in terms of its art'. He had been drawn to Venice on a visit in 1950. 'I don't know why I decided on that theme. It was just pragmatic. I wanted to do something on my own, I liked the city, it seemed a wonderful place to make a movie. I didn't know anything about Venetian painting, or the history of Venice as such. I hardly knew anything about the place of Venice in the grand scheme of things.'

Ivory's concept of the film changed when he returned to USC with his footage and began to collaborate with the documentary film-maker Lester Novros, his faculty advisor. The film developed into a painters' view of Venice. 'At a certain point, painters were no longer depicting Venice as a chronicle of its great events. In the 18th century and after, Venice itself became the subject. I was evidently interested then in the idea of an ancient civilisation in decay. The 18th century interested me most, Guardi and Longhi.'*

The draft finally caught up with him and after a comfortable two years as an NCO in the US Army's Special Services posted to the German headquarters of the Second Armored Division, during which he worked as a producer's assistant on soldier shows (and, at the Army's expense, broadened his acquaintance with European cities), Ivory returned to the United States and resumed editing *Venice*, the shape of which he now more clearly saw. He shot additional footage in museums on both the East and West coasts, concentrating on Guardi, Saul Steinberg (with whom he became friends), Whistler and Longhi. Dissatisfied with his first narrator, Ivory found a second, more tried practitioner, Alexander Scourby. The film was finished, at which point Ivory learned his first salutary lesson about the nature of film distribution.

'I remember the first few people I showed the film to – it was like later on

James Ivory, Satyajit Ray, during the making of 'Shakespeare Wallah'

JI: Like our later feature film *Savages*, *Venice: Theme and Variations* has no Golden Age. We go straight from the early Renaissance of Carpaccio and Gentile Bellini, to Guardi, skipping Titian, Tintoretto and Veronese. Rather a magnificent omission, as somebody pointed out. I don't think I much appreciated Titian and Tintoretto. They didn't in any case show Venice as a city; neither did Veronese, though his big compositions, even if they were religious allegories, summed up the high life in Venice at its most opulent period. I did try to shoot The Wedding Feast at Cana, but it was scrappy, just close-ups – I didn't have enough light or space to show the whole picture – so in the end I cut it.

James Ivory and Shashi Kapoor during the shooting of 'The Householder'

JI: There was again the dissatisfaction with the original narrator, an American actor with a heavy, too sincere voice. This is when I found Saeed Jaffrey, acting in Lorca's *Blood Wedding* in Greenwich Village, and he introduced me to his wife Madhur.

when you showed your film to Hollywood executives, and they were busy on the telephone, and going in and out. Exactly like that. But these were distributors of *art* films, who you wouldn't suppose had that many irons in the fire that they would *have* to take a call in the middle of a half-hour film? In the end, *Venice* was taken by the reputable Film Images of New York; it was favourably noticed in the *New York Times*. 'It ended where my teachers at USC would have liked it, in audio-visual education.'

Ivory's new interest in Italian 18th-century painters led him to a San Francisco print-dealer, Raymond Lewis, in whose gallery Ivory discovered, spread out on a table, an array of Indian miniature paintings. He knew from his experiences with *Venice* that they could be photographed with effect, and the notion of his second film, *The Sword and the Flute*, was born. The notion had novelty to recommend it. The Western interest in Indian music had hardly begun (though Ivory was among the early admirers of Ali Akbar Khan and Ravi Shankar whose music he was later to use in *The Sword and the Flute*), and published criticism of Indian art was sparse. Again financed by his father, who was doubtful of his son's career but gratified that *Venice* had found a distributor, Ivory scoured public and private collections on both sides of America, educating himself meanwhile in Indian art and history. After his original cameraman, Mindaugis Bagdon, a fellow-student from USC, had been drafted, he became his own photographer, and subsequently his own editor.

Composed entirely of shots of paintings, *The Sword and the Flute* is a concise history of the two principal strands of Indian miniature painting, the Mogul and the Rajput. What makes this introductory art history lesson more compelling than Ivory's Venetian survey is the element of surprise. Venice is familiar to Western eyes; Indian miniatures are not. Later, Ivory was to introduce Western audiences for the first time to the palaces where these paintings were housed, and the shock of the new was as great. In *Venice*, the waters of the lagoon lapped the ancient stones; in *The Sword and the Flute*, thanks to some cunning editing, a tiger leapt from the jungle. One also senses in the Indian film Ivory's excitement: the feeling that here was a subject which would animate the viewer. This was no thesis film.*

After a screening of *The Sword and the Flute* at a New York party, the head of the Asia Society, Paul Sherbert, took Ivory aside and asked if he would like to go to India and make a film of his own devising about Delhi. Ivory said he would, and Sherbert undertook to approach Mrs John D. Rockefeller 3rd, one of the society's patrons. Meanwhile, Ivory occupied himself on a project with Saul Steinberg. 'In the 1950s, Steinberg drew a series of views of America, of its cities and landscapes. These suggested a cross-country trip to me. In many drawings you would see the steering wheel of a car, the rear-view mirror – almost like shots in a film – and someone looking into the mirror, the road receding into the background and the road unwinding ahead. I tried to make something of this, shot thousands of feet of 16mm film. I wanted Steinberg to draw directly for the camera, so we'd see the nib of the pen and the black ink flowing out. But before we began experimenting, he decided that, from his point of view, the exercise would be mechanical. He didn't care for the camera peering over his shoulder. I don't think in the end he would have found it mechanical or boring, but I couldn't very well force him to do this.'

Mrs Rockefeller advanced $20,000 (Ivory: 'a lot of money') and Ivory departed for India with a commission to make two films, one on Delhi and another on Afghanistan. (Ivory shot several thousand feet of 16mm film around Kabul but the Afghan film itself was never completed.) He worked in and around Delhi from October 1959 to May 1960. 'I would just gather up anything that looked interesting,' Ivory said. 'I shot in Agra which in itself has nothing to do with Delhi. The Mogul buildings in Agra, however, do have something to do with the Mogul buildings in Delhi.' The Asia Society wanted a record of Indian dancers; so, despite having no sound equipment, Ivory travelled to South India and shot this footage.* He took a summer trip to Afghanistan. 'When I returned the monsoon was on. Everything had changed, everything was green and kind of frothy looking. By this time I had very much fallen in love with India and had many Indian friends. He had met Ruth Jhabvala briefly. On his return to New York, Ivory found life pale and uninteresting. He wanted to go back to India to shoot some more footage for the Delhi film – *The Delhi Way* – though by this time the Asia Society grant was all used up. 'Fortunately, I was only back in New York a few months when I met Ismail.' *The Delhi Way* was eventually finished after *The Householder*.

THE WRITER

Ruth Prawer Jhabvala was born Ruth Prawer in Cologne on 7 May 1927. Her father, a solicitor, had come to Germany during the First World War to escape conscription in Poland; her mother was German-born, but her mother's father had emigrated from Russia – probably, his granddaughter has said, also to escape conscription. (I am indebted for much of the following to a lecture given in Edinburgh in April 1979 by Ruth Jhabvala, in acceptance of a Neil Gunn International Fellowship, and published in *Blackwood's Magazine* in July 1979). Her maternal grandfather was the cantor in Cologne's largest synagogue; the family was comfortable, assimilated, well-respected. Ruth Jhabvala's most basic memory is of the family grouped at a piano listening to her grandfather clear his throat in preparation for a song. 'From the kitchen the delicate flavour of a particular type of round little tea cake that only my grandmother knew how to bake,' Ruth Jhabvala said. 'There were aunts and uncles, all well settled, all German patriots, all life-loving, full of energy, bourgeois virtues

JI: These were all well-known Indian dancers, though perhaps not then (1960) quite the stars they would soon become. Mine is solely a visual record of them in their twenties and thirties; unfortunately there is no sound: Biju Maharaj, the greatest Kathak dancer, seductively whirling and stamping in the *Diwani Khas* of the Red Fort in Delhi; Kamala Laxman, doing *Bharta Natyam* on the sands in front of the sea temple at Mahabalipuram; and Indrani Rehman's *Kuchipudi* at the Qutb Minar. Everything is fine – the dancing, the dramatic backdrops – but it is all in mime: expressive in the way a Victorian photograph of Indian dancers can sometimes be expressive, but mute.

FIRST INFLUENCES

As adults, Ismail Merchant, James Ivory and Ruth Jhabvala recalled the films which they had seen in childhood and adolescence and each picked five which had impressed them vividly. *Shama* is included by Merchant as a single representative of the films of Nimmi, and *Swiss Miss* by Ruth Jhabvala as a representative of those by Laurel and Hardy. *Gone With the Wind* was a favourite of all three.

James Ivory: 'They say that you are what you eat, and in the movies the three of us saw on our different continents, what we were consuming so avidly seems to have been the cinematic equivalent to a lot of ice-cream, crackerjacks, *jelabis* and Viennese pastry – but with a satisfying dash of vinegar when we got to Bette Davis and Clare Booth Luce. When one grows older, of course, one goes on a diet and learns to choose more refined delicacies. There's a lot of picking at what's on the plate: no more innocent gorging.'

Ismail Merchant: 'I remember, in *Mela*, Dilip Kumar and Nargis first meeting in a village. Dilip Kumar had a sort of mating call – a song – it was a Hindu couplet: "Dharti ko akash pukare – Aaja, Aaja Prem Diwane…" It was like the Earth calling out to the Sky. It all ended in tragedy, and we couldn't accept it and cried and cried.'

ISMAIL MERCHANT

SHAMA (1961)
India: director, Lekhraj Bhahakri
Nimmi

SAMSON AND DELILAH (1949)
U.S.A.: director, Cecil B. DeMille
Victor Mature

JAMES IVORY

GONE WITH THE WIND (1939)
U.S.A.: director, Victor Fleming
Vivien Leigh, Olivia de Havilland

THE WIZARD OF OZ (1939)
U.S.A.: director, Victor Fleming
Judy Garland and friends

RUTH JHABVALA

SWISS MISS (1938)
U.S.A.: director, John Blystone
Stan Laurel, Oliver Hardy

IT HAPPENED ONE NIGHT (1934)
U.S.A.: director, Frank Capra
Clark Gable, Claudette Colbert

MAN HOLIDAY (1953)
.A.: director, William Wyler
Irey Hepburn

REAR WINDOW (1954)
U.S.A.: director, Alfred Hitchcock
Grace Kelly, James Stewart

MELA (1949)
India: director, S.U. Suny
Dilip Kumar, Nargis

RIE ANTOINETTE (1938)
A.: director, W. S. Van Dyke
ma Shearer, Joseph Schildkraut

THE MUMMY'S HAND (1940)
U.S.A.: director, Christy Cabanne
Tom Tyler

DRUMS ALONG THE MOHAWK (1939)
U.S.A.: director, John Ford
Western perils

HAT (1935)
A.: director, Mark Sandrich
Astaire, Ginger Rogers

THE WOMEN (1939)
U.S.A.: director, George Cukor
Rosalind Russell (right)

LES ENFANTS DU PARADIS (1945)
France: director, Marcel Carné
Jean-Louis Barrault (left)

and pleasures, celebrating every kind of festival – all the Jewish holidays, of course, but what they really liked was New Year's Eve and, especially, the annual Cologne carnival and masked ball. We all had costumes made for that every year; one year I was a chimney-sweep, and another a Viennese pastrycook. All this would be in the early 1930s – up to, but not including, 1933.'

She became a writer – or at least sensed she could write and that it brought her immense pleasure – from the moment she sat down to her first German composition, *Der Hase*, the Hare. It was, she said, her destiny. 'I read everything there was to read. I wrote and wrote and had drawers full of unfinished novels, unfinished stories and unfinished plays. As a boy, my brother Siegbert, who is now Professor of German Literature at Oxford, was very literary: he read all the German Classics, which I didn't.' The Jewish writer Sholem Ash was, it seemed, somehow related, perhaps by marriage – 'We certainly all came from the same town in Poland.' There were, however, no particular literary influences in Ruth Jhabvala's immediate family; on the other hand, she did not come from a background where writing was anything strange.

Ruth Jhabvala has spoken of her 'disinheritance' as both a person and a writer: it was the title of her Neil Gunn lecture. 'I don't feel like talking much about 1933 and after. Everyone knows what happened to German Jews first and other European Jews after. Our family was no exception. One by one all the aunts and uncles emigrated – to France, Holland, what was then Palestine, the United States… My immediate family – that is my Polish father, my mother, my brother and myself – were the last to emigrate, and also the only ones to go to England. This was 1939. I have slurred over the years 1933 to 1939, from when I was six to twelve. They should have been my most formative years; maybe they were, I don't know. Together with the early happy German-Jewish bourgeois family years – 1927 to 1933 – they should be that profound well of memory and experience (childhood and ancestral) from which as a writer I should have drawn. I never have. I have never written about those years. To tell you the truth, until today [April 1979] I've never mentioned them. Never spoken about them to anyone. I don't know why not. I suppose they are the beginning of my disinheritance – the way they are for other writers of their inheritance.'

Within a week of landing in England, Ruth Jhabvala began to write in English, having previously only the little English learned at school in Cologne, and was soon not only writing in English but about English subjects. 'I have to live in a place to write about it. I actually have to be there, to look out of the window and see the weather. When I think that a writer like Joyce carried Dublin everywhere, wherever he went. He unfolded it and unfolded it and it was always his interior landscape. I don't have anything like that, unfortunately. There is a storehouse of memories, but I want to be right there, to be

'Fanny Elssler'

26

triggered right there. I want to hear the speech rhythms of everybody around me.' She wrote about the life she saw in the Midlands. 'I first went to Coventry, then was evacuated to Leamington Spa to two maiden sisters and their caretaker father.' In 1940, she rejoined her parents who had bought a house in North London (her father gave up the law and went into business as a wholesaler of ladies' goods) and was sent to Hendon County School. She was later admitted to Queen Mary College, London University, and took a degree in English.

'England opened out the world of literature for me; what other writers have experienced and set down. Not really having a world of my own, I made up for my disinheritance by absorbing the world of others. The more regional, the more deeply rooted a writer was, the more I loved them: George Eliot, Thomas Hardy, Charles Dickens. The landscape, their childhood memories, became mine. I adopted them passionately. But I was equally passionate to adopt, for instance, the landscape of Marcel Proust, of James Joyce, of Henry James, of the great Russians – Tolstoy, Turgenev, Chekhov (the noble roll-call). Whatever author I read last, I was ready to become a figure in that particular landscape. It was as if I had no sense of my own – besides no country of my own – but only theirs.'

For someone who was later to spend much of her working life closely involved in film-making, Ruth Jhabvala does not class herself as a film enthusiast. As a child and a teenager she saw films with no greater frequency than her contemporaries – 'say once or twice a week'. And she does not claim they greatly influenced her. In a letter to James Ivory (18 September 1982), she had this to say about her early moviegoing: 'Once I started thinking about films I had seen in early years, I found I remembered better than I thought. Here they are in chronological order: Charlie Chaplin, Laurel and Hardy, and Shirley Temple – those must have been the earliest; a German film called *Fanny Elssler* [1937] about a famous Viennese dancer who had an affair with some royal figure – very stirring and touching; then the films in Holland dubbed or subtitled into Dutch [being a Jew, cinemagoing in Germany was forbidden to Ruth Prawer after 1936 but she saw some films on visits to relatives in Holland] – all Hollywood comedies like *Top Hat* and *It Happened One Night*. Then England during the war: the very first I remember seeing in England in English was *The Great Waltz*, then *The Women* and *Beau Geste* – these were on Saturday mornings in Coventry and Leamington; then in London *Gone With the Wind*, *Mrs Miniver* and *Henry V*; and my first all-time favourite French art film (at the Everyman, Hampstead), *Un Carnet de Bal*; and later *Les Enfants du Paradis*. All these were during or maybe just after the war – but only just, because I don't seem to remember much between 1945 and 1951.'

In 1949, Ruth Prawer met a young Indian, C. S. H. Jhabvala. He had just completed an architectural degree in London and was on the point of

Ruth Prawer Jhabvala at Kasauli during the shooting of 'Shakespeare Wallah'

Ruth Jhabvala, James Ivory, Ismail Merchant

returning home. He asked her to wait for him; she did; he returned and they were married in June 1951 in a North London register office. They left England for Delhi, where he had what was to become a successful architectural practice, and for the next fifteen years Ruth Jhabvala remained in India, voluntarily cut off from a Western heritage which she was for a long time never sure she actually possessed. She had three daughters and continued to write with her customary dedication. She later remarked, 'I don't *try* to sit down every day to write, I sit down.'

In India, Ruth Jhabvala's cinemagoing was sporadic. 'I do have memories of Hindi films, like the early Raj Kapoor ones, and whatever Satyajit Ray ones I could get to in Delhi – usually at 9 a.m. and in Bengali without subtitles.' Reflecting on these films and those of her childhood and youth, she wrote to Ivory: 'Two things strike me – most of them have a show-biz glitter even when they're not actually about entertainment (though many of them are – like Fanny Elssler who was a dancer, *The Great Waltz* about Strauss and Vienna, *Les Enfants du Paradis* about actors, and *Un Carnet de Bal* about a dance hall). And the second thing I notice is how often I couldn't understand the language and was left without subtitles, as in the Dutch, Hindi and Bengali films. In the beginning in England, I probably couldn't understand the American dialogue too well either; and when I first saw foreign films, I had difficulty reading the subtitles because of weak eyesight. So it is no wonder I always feel dialogue in films is not important and am so cheerfully ready to cut out huge chunks of it.'

'I still can't talk about the first impact India made on my innocent – meaning blank and unprepared – mind and sense,' Ruth Jhabvala said in her Neil Gunn lecture. 'To try to express it would make me stutter... I entered a world of sensuous delights that perhaps children – other children – enter. That way India was – remains till today – my childhood (although I was twenty-four when I went there). I don't know why this was so. Was it in reaction to the bleakness and deprivations of my own childhood – Nazi

Germany and then wartime blitzed London (those days and nights spent in damp air-raid shelters, and queueing for matches and margarine)? Or did it go farther, and was it that whatever was Oriental within me – I mean, through my being Jewish – was opening up a buried ancestral memory? I don't know, but whatever it was, it was very strong and lasted for years… The smells and sights and sounds of India – the mango and jasmine on hot nights – the rich spiced food – the vast sky – the sight of dawn and dusk – the birds flying about – the ruins – the music – I've tried to write about it; I've spent years writing about it. At that time I loved everything there: yes – to my shame I have to say – even the beggars, the poverty, they didn't seem to bother me then; they seemed right somehow, a part of life that had been taken out of the West (like death, which was also always present in India, carried on a bier in front of my window down to the burning ghats, or the vultures swooping over something indescribable in a ditch). It was life as one read about it in the Bible: whole, I thought; pure, I thought.'

Between 1955 and 1960, Ruth Jhabvala published four books in England. The first two with Allen & Unwin, *To Whom She Will* and *Esmond in India*, and the others with John Murray, whose author she was to remain, *The Nature of Passion* and *The Householder*. In 1961 came the telephone call from Ismail Merchant.

The Creation of Woman (1960)

p.c–Trident Films. *exec. p*–IM. *d/sc*–Charles Schwep. *ph*–Wheaton Galentine. *a.d*–Jim McIntyre. *choreo*–Bhaskar Roy Chaudhuri. *narration*–Saeed Jaffrey. *cast* Bhaskar Roy Chaudhuri, Dinu, Anjali Devi. 14 mins. (35mm).

Venice: Theme and Variations (1957)

p.c/p/d/sc/ph–JI. In colour. *addit. ph/ed*–Stelios Roccos. *narrator*–Alexander Scourby. *p. collaboration*–The Museum of Fine Arts, Boston; the California Palace of the Legion of Honor, San Francisco; the Gallerie dell' Accademia, Venice; the Los Angeles County Museum; the Metropolitan Museum of Art; the National Gallery of Art, Washington, D.C.; the Procuratoria di San Marco, Venice; the San Diego Art Museum; the Byzantine Society of Records and the Byzantine Chorale (under the direction of Frank Desby); Sileno Corsini; the Curtis Publishing Company, Philadelphia; Harper & Brothers, New York; Lester Novros; Anita M. Peabody, Saul Steinberg; Mrs Diego Suarez; the University of Southern California, Department of Cinema. 28 mins. (16mm).

The Sword and the Flute (1959)

p.c/p/d/sc–JI. *ph*–Mindaugis Bagdon. In colour. *ed*–JI. *m*–Ustad Ali Akbar Khan, Ravi Shankar, T. Visvanathan, Chatur Lal, D. R. Parvatikar. *sd. rec*–Rolf Epstein. *special p. assistance*–Raymond E. Lewis. *narrator*–Saeed Jaffrey. *p. collaboration*–The Museum of Fine Arts, Boston; the Freer Gallery, Washington, D.C.; the Metropolitan Museum of Art; Hyman Bloom; Richard Bock; Charles Campbell; Mr and Mrs William P. Cleary; Dr and Mrs D. I. Elterman; Mrs Charles Fabri; Roger Malek; Robert Marquis; Anita M. Peabody; James Rubin. 24 mins. (16mm).

The Delhi Way (1964)

p.c–The Asia Society, New York. *p/d*–JI. *asst. d*–Toon Ghose. *sc/ph*–JI. In colour. *ed*–JI. *m*–Ustad Vilayat Khan; Pandit Shantaprasad. *addit. m. performers*–Abhayankar, Bala Bhau, G.S. Sachdev, Dinanath, Radhakanto Nandy, Virmal Biswas. *p. assistants*–Maniza Boga, Daphne Ghose, Ratna Fabri, Charles O. Hyman, Saeed Jaffrey, Madhur Jaffrey, Michael Jorrin, Jennifer Kapoor, Awtar Kaul, IM, Subrata Mitra, Robert Skelton. *narrator*–Leo Genn. *p. collaboration*–The Royal Library, Windsor Castle; the National Film Archive, the British Film Institute; the Department of Archeology, the Government of India; the India Office Library; the British Museum; Stuart C. Welch Jr. 45 mins. (16mm).

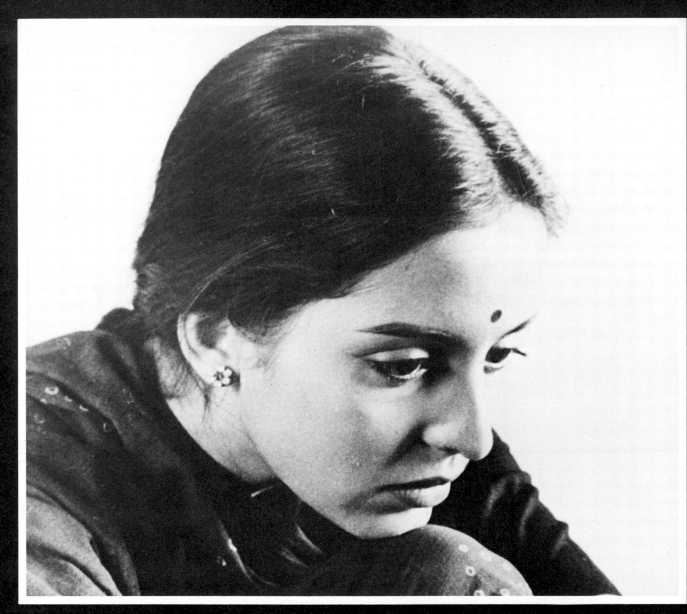

Leela Naidu

Chapter Two

AN EXPERIENCE OF INDIA

THE HOUSEHOLDER

Shashi Kapoor, Leela Naidu, Durga Khote
Locations: Delhi, Mehrauli, Ghaziabad
Shooting: March to August 1962
Premiere: New York, October 1963

A country wedding. Young Prem, a lowly Hindi teacher at a boys' college in Delhi, consoles his friend the groom, who is about to be joined to a girl he hardly knows, with an account – told in flashback – of the early days of his own marriage. His untidy wife, Indu, could not cook to his satisfaction; money worries preyed on him; he felt little more than a boy himself, a second-class BA and unable to stand up to the mean college principal. When Indu became pregnant, Prem's own doting mother was summoned. Indu, however, felt her place usurped and soon departed for her family. Prem subsequently fell in with some Westerners, but their attempts to divert his present worries with thoughts of higher spiritual matters only intensified his loneliness and uncertainty. Eventually, finding herself as lonely as her husband, Indu came back and the expulsion of the mother-in-law was effected. Distrust blossomed into love. The new groom remains sunk in gloom; Prem and Indu, however, return home at peace with one another.

'There is no pillar of virtue heroine, no dyed-in-wool villain,' said one Indian review of the film of *The Householder* (*Montage*, Winter 1963). 'They are all slightly perplexed human creatures trying to grapple with hard fact and ... to retain a warmth of feeling without resorting to banalities and implausible melodrama. There are no clichés of virtue threatened by hipswaying enchantresses ... It has no happy ending as such, with the 100 piece invisible orchestra working overtime.' And another in the Indian *Screen* (17 August 1964): 'The

'The Householder': Shashi Kapoor, Durga Khote

JI: I was surprised to hear, when I first arrived in India, that Ray had made two other features between episodes of the Apu Trilogy – *The Philosopher's Stone* and *The Music Room*. From the description of the latter I knew it was something I *had* to see. Ray is very accessible and I simply called him up when I arrived in Calcutta and told him what I wanted. He invited me to meet him in a coffee house and I went there and saw this very tall man in the gloom looking somewhat apprehensive. He was waiting to hear whether *Devi* had been passed by the censors, who were then seeing it in a nearby cinema. He was afraid that this story of religious superstition might be found offensive and have to be cut, but while we were having our coffee, someone from his staff came in to say that all had gone well. He did run *The Music Room* for me, reluctantly. He felt that it was not up to the mark technically and seemed surprised that people were speaking well of it in Delhi, where I'd been told about it. He translated the dialogue for me when he thought I was missing something important and when the film was over and I jumped up and excitedly told him how much I'd liked it, again he seemed doubtful about it and spoke deprecatingly when I said I hoped it would come to the West, where I was sure people would be crazy about it, too. It started westward finally, via the Moscow Film Festival, where naturally it was regarded as decadent, and opened in New York in 1963. Almost 20 years later the film made it to Paris, where it was a smash success, running for months and months – I think it's still running there, and it's certainly on a lot of filmgoers' Best Films List, including mine.

characters are all made excellent targets of satire. In fact it is sarcasm more than satire that predominates … However, this wealth of sarcasm being too subdued is bound to go over the head of the Indian cine-goer, accustomed as he is to loud melodrama and broad comedy.'

The Householder was Ruth Jhabvala's fourth novel; and, in 1962, she was about to publish her fifth, *Get Ready for Battle*. 'I was already getting restless,' she said. 'Maybe I would have started writing plays if Jim and Ismail hadn't come. I was in a rut, I wanted some new form. We certainly didn't know anything. I mean, I didn't know anything. I hadn't seen any films, because I had been in India since 1951. They said, "Why don't you write the screenplay of *The Householder* ?" And I said, "All right." Nobody told me it was different from other kinds of writing – and to tell the truth it isn't.' *The Householder*, billed by Merchant as 'the first Indo-American co-production in Hindi and English,' went before the camera in Delhi in March 1962. (Merchant Ivory Productions, which co-ordinated the funding, was not in fact incorporated until June 1963 in New York.) With the exception of Ray's *Kanchenjunga* (1962), it was, Ivory believes, the first Indian feature to be shot entirely on location. It was also, to an extent, shot on the wing. There was no art director as such, and the iron bedstead in the opening scene was exactly as Merchant found it on the roof of the house belonging to his friend Inder Narayan. The house was offered as a location. Friends, and friends of friends, were co-opted: the late R.G. Anand, the business partner of C.S.H. Jhabvala, translated the screenplay for the simultaneous Hindi version.

Ivory had first met Satyajit Ray in 1960 during the making of *The Delhi Way*, when he sought out the director in the hope of being shown *The Music Room*. Earlier, in San Francisco while working on *The Sword and the Flute*, Ivory had seen *Pather Panchali* (1955). 'I had never seen a film that so thrilled me. It was not just the story, poor struggling Indians in a village in Bengal, it was the presentation: the beauty of the images, the intoxicating sounds, the music, the lyricism of it. Rather in the same kind of way that *The River* had worked on me, though I didn't know it: a seamless whole, just to be experienced like a piece of music. (The first thing I heard in *The River* was the sitar music played by the man who was later to be my cameraman, Subrata Mitra.) I was equally bowled over by *The Music Room* [1958], which remains one of my favourite movies.* Ray later invited me to watch the shooting of *Two Daughters* [1961], by which time we were sort of friendly.'

Several members of Ray's regular crew, including his long-time cameraman Subrata Mitra, who was to work with MIP on their first four films, came from Calcutta to Delhi for *The Householder*. 'Without Ray's presence there was a great deal of rivalry and it wasn't always a happy group,' Ivory said. 'By and large though they were all very helpful to me, kept me from many of the mistakes a beginner makes. Mitra had by that time made so many films with Ray that, like most cameramen, he had a sense of what will cut and he wouldn't let me do anything wrong in that sense.'*

The screenplay was written in about ten days. 'Ruth read us the whole script,' said Merchant. 'She kept on reading and we kept on laughing.' 'I'm very fond of *The Householder*,' Ruth Jhabvala said, 'even though it's so naive and full of the most awful mistakes. I like writing dialogue, and I wrote masses and masses. I slashed it down, but even then I found I had far too much. With the next two films I became rather inhibited about giving the characters anything to say. This mistake perhaps came to a head in *The Guru*. But then I went round again and gave them a bit more. But I know it was because of *The Householder*: I saw that in film dialogue does work differently.' 'Ruth wrote the script from memory,' Ivory said. 'The script originally lacked one scene from the book which I asked her to put back. The one where Prem confronts the schoolmaster, Mr Chadda, and asks "Why have you embarrassed me in front of my pupils?" It ends with the schoolmaster turning the tables on him. Prem backs out apologising. I remember when we did that too, it was one of those long takes, I think the first I ever did. It was necessary for that old actor to remember his lines, which he didn't...'

Halfway through the shooting, the money, which had come from Ivory's father and several private sources in Bombay, ran out. 'We went to Bombay and started making the rounds,' Merchant said. 'The financiers saw the first few reels of edited film, and said "No, this isn't going to make money." We applied to the Film Finance Corporation. There was a man there, Mr Kotak, with the gold bullion market... he hadn't seen a film for 40 years. He thought it was anti-Indian, making jokes about Indian mothers-in-law. Our application was refused. We were introduced to a moneylender. We wanted $25,000. He said he would give us $20,000 and deduct $5,000 as interest first. We were devastated. It was pouring with rain. I was driving the car and crying and saying "There is no one in life to help you when you are young." It was a merciless world. We went to our first investors, and at that time one of them – he had recently opened a cinema in Bombay – had just had a big hit with *The Guns of Navarone*. He was in a great frame of mind to put up some money. We showed the reels to an American executive from Columbia Pictures, who was visiting Bombay, and he liked them very much. "When it's completed bring it to New York and maybe Columbia will take it." Somehow, with these friends, and with Jim's father coming up with some additional money, we finished the film.' The cost was some $125,000 for the two versions.

The film was cut in Bombay, but seemed to the makers unwieldy. Trunks and trunks of film were then transported to Calcutta. 'Ray saw it and liked it,' Ivory said. 'We asked him how we could improve it. He immediately offered to recut it for us, provided we just let him do what he wanted, then if we didn't like it we could put back the bits he'd cut. He got through the whole film in three

'The Householder':
**Hariendernath
Chattopadayaya and Shashi
Kapoor**

JI: It was only when the crew arrived at the Old Delhi station that I was sure the film was going to be made. Up to then I hadn't quite believed it. When I saw the mountains of equipment and other gear and other personal baggage being piled up on the station platform, and the army of coolies lugging it out of the train, I felt both joy and apprehension: it had all got so *serious* suddenly. To this day, perhaps superstitiously, I look forward to the arrival of the camera cases, in their impressive array of shiny silver boxes, which seem to have proliferated over the decades. Then I know the film is truly happening.

'The Householder': Leela
Naidu

JI: Ray recut the film in an editing
room in the studio at Tollygunj, a
suburb of Calcutta, where he worked
a lot in those days. Dulal Dutta, his
regular editor, did the actual work,
while Ray stood behind the Moviola
crying out 'Cut!' at the points where
material was to go. This took some
getting used to – not so much losing
sequences, but the explosive force of
the command which blew them
away.

days.* It was Ray who thought of the framing flashback, which, he said,
contained one inelegant feature in that there was a flashback within a
flashback. Indu remembering her girlhood, he didn't like that. But there
wasn't much we could do about it, and the scene was nice itself. All the
wedding came at the end, in the first version and in the book, shots and shots of
the wedding, the procession and all that business on the roof. That was
something we learned the hard way. You can't have a scene like that at the end
of a film. Once the story's told, it's told, that's that. I think that was what was
bothering Ruth, and probably me too. In the book the wedding and the
expedition to the country was a few lines; in the film it was ten minutes of quite
good footage. We didn't want to lose that footage, and in the end much of it was
saved.'

The Householder is at its best when detailing the specifics of everyday life; and,
despite Ruth Jhabvala's protest about her inaccuracies, several of the Indian
critics in fact confirmed the acuteness of her eye for telling incidentals such as
the scene in which Prem (played by Shashi Kapoor, a rising star from a famous
acting family) buys a silk blouse piece for his wife – in fact it goes to his covetous
mother – only to be given a yard of unasked for advice from some passing
women, who unashamedly pry into and giggle at his obvious inexperience in
such womanly matters. The details of Prem and Indu's home seem exact and
complete; and the shading of their lives – her sudden playfulness, his no less
childish exasperation; his sententiousness, her silent acquiescence – suggests
a modest universality. Western critics, who later responded to the film with
enthusiasm, all, it seemed, delighted in recounting the film's touching and
humorous detailing; in pointing up its irony rather than its 'sarcasm'. One
reason that the Western critics responded enthusiastically was that this was
India filtered by a discerning Western eye, made both believable and
comprehensible.

What chiefly endures in *The Householder* is the freshness of two young players
finding their moment. Shashi Kapoor, one of the charter members of the
Merchant Ivory family of actors and technicians, and the part-French actress
Leela Naidu, who played Indu with a singularly self-possessed intensity, both
convey – along with much else – youth's disarming lack of perspective. Time
has not yet really caught up with them. This fact is highlighted in the comic
scene in which Prem watches in agony as his pregnant wife disgraces him at the
tea party given by the principal's ghastly wife by popping cake after cake into
her mouth. In her innocence she doesn't understand why her greed is giving
her husband pain; and in his innocence he doesn't understand why she has a
craving for sweets.

Less successful are the generalities: the clash of East and West (though it is
less a clash than a plain failure to communicate) in the scenes in which Prem
visits the distinctly unrooted household of truth-seekers. Unlike his day-

'The Householder': Leela
Naidu, Shashi Kapoor,
returning from wedding

dreams of the film star Nimmi, which were at least grounded in a certain sort of tangible fantasy, the product of the Bombay film land, the fantasies of the Westerners seemed utterly apart from Prem's circumscribed workaday world. Phoney though the Westerners are meant to be, their phoneyness does not in the end mesh with the somehow more authentic (though no less put-on) pomposity of such characters as the obese principal and the self-satisfied older teacher who occupies the other, better ordered end of Prem's classroom. 'Not so phoney,' Ivory said, 'as just badly acted, or more to the point, badly cast. We might have used the Kendals then. We already knew them, but instead chose unprofessional actors out of local amateur drama groups. Ernest Castaldo, who played Prem's American friend, was a professional Broadway actor, principally a singer and dancer, far from the stolid, graceless Teuton of the novel, but at least he could act. With time I might have toned the others down, or toned them up a bit, but I didn't know how.' In their next film, Merchant, Ivory and Ruth Jhabvala brought East and West together in a far more organic and telling manner.

p.c–MIP. p–IM. d–JI. p. co-ordinator–Salien Dutt. p. controller–Riaz Hafizka. p. managers–Bhanu Ghosh, N. Kabir. asst. d–Prayag Raaj. sc–RPJ based on her own novel. translation Hindi version–R.G. Anand. ph–Subrata Mitra. asst. camera–Fatik Mazumdar, Joy Mitra, Shankar Chatterji. ed–Pran Mehra; (asst.) Raja Ram Khotle. m–Ustad Ali Akbar Khan. m. asst–Jai Dev. incidental m–Jyotirindra Moitra; Vanraj Bhatia. cost–Bettina Gill. make-up–Nath Grover. sd. rec–Sujeet Sarkar, N. Mehta. sd. re-rec–Kaushik. cast–Shashi Kapoor (Prem Sagar), Leela Naidu (Indu), Durga Khote (Prem's Mother), Achla Sachdev (Mrs Saigal, the landlady), Hariendernath Chattopadayaya (Mr Chadda, the rival teacher), Pahari Sanyal (the Swami), Romesh Thapar (Mr Khanna, the principal), Walter King (the Professor), Patsy Dance (Kitty), Indu Lele (Mrs Khanna), Prayag Raaj (Raj, Prem's worldwise friend), Pincho Kapoor (Mr Saigal, the landlord), Praveen Paul and Usha Amin (Ladies at the tea party), Shama Beg (Raj's Wife), Pro-Sen (Sohanlal), Jabeen Jalil (Bobo), Ernest Castaldo (Ernest). 101 mins. (35 mm).

Shashi Kapoor, Felicity
Kendal

SHAKESPEARE WALLAH

Shashi Kapoor, Felicity Kendal, Madhur Jaffrey
Locations: Kasauli, Simla, Alwar, Lucknow, Bombay
Shooting: September 1964 to January 1965
Premiere: Berlin Film Festival, June 1965

'Shakespeare Wallah': Utpal
Dutt

An English girl, the junior member of a company of travelling players, falls in love with a wealthy young Indian. He, however, is already half claimed by a Bombay film star. Her parents, believing they are acting for the best, despatch her to England. The action unfolds with melancholy regret and melancholy inevitability against the panorama of India.

There is a palpable reality to the interaction – an acceptance and resignation born of long acquaintance – between the English and Indian members of the Buckingham Players, the travelling company, which specialises in versatile adaptations of the English classics but whose fortunes have progressively declined in post-Independence India. Prem was condescended to by his Western friends; they spoke at, not to him. In *Shakespeare Wallah*, however, when the Maharaja at whose palace the players first arrive regales his dinner guests with a rendition of 'Let us sit upon the ground/And tell sad stories of the death of kings', one realises at once that the two senior Buckinghams, the girl's parents, who belong to a generation which would never dream of showing anything less than complete and judicious politeness,

36

are sufficiently steeped in Indian manners that they would, equally, never give any sign that they were being condescended to. (Also they require the Maharaja's patronage in a way that Prem never required the help of his Western friends.)

The Buckinghams, with their regular school visits (and the film opens with an incongruous scene from an open-air performance of Sheridan's *The Critic* against an ornamental pond and before an audience of unsuitably beflanneled boys), are consequently aware of their role – now, it seems, no longer wanted, though no one can quite bring himself to say so – as dispensers of truth, the truth of literature. But, unlike the Westerners of *The Householder*, they have come to understand that India is for them a place of impermanence. They know they should depart, the next scene, as it were, having begun, but they can't. The movies – the 'Bombay talkies' of MIP's fourth film – are impinging with a sort of bottomless comic vulgarity outside the experience of the staid Mr and Mrs Buckingham. The old India, the Gleneagles Hotel in half-timbered mock-Tudor Simla where they have lodged, year in and year out, is losing custom, its wine rack is dismally empty, and, one knows, is never likely to be replenished. *Shakespeare Wallah*, however, is not so much a reflection of the end of the Raj, as of the fate of its individual idiosyncratic camp followers.

Ivory began thinking about a proposed film about a group of Indian travelling players before the shooting of *The Householder*. At the same time he was lent a diary kept for a few years after 1947 by Shashi Kapoor's father-in-law, Geoffrey Kendal. This described the vicissitudes of Shakespeariana, a troupe of Anglo-Indian travelling players, led by Geoffrey Kendal and his wife, Laura Liddel. Ruth Jhabvala, who had seen the Kendals perform in Delhi in the 50s, was like Ivory intrigued by the diary, although she did not, when she came to write the script of *Shakespeare Wallah*, draw directly upon it. 'But', Ruth Jhabvala said 'the Kendals travelled throughout India, just as the Buckinghams did in the film. They did live in the sort of places one sees in the film; they trekked all over and went on trains and slept on station platforms, doing Shakespeare all the way.'

Unlike the script of *The Householder*, a straightforward adaptation, the script of *Shakespeare Wallah* was developed largely through a correspondence between Ivory in New York and Ruth Jhabvala in Delhi. Ivory would propose incidents which had caught his fancy, and which he wanted included, and Ruth Jhabvala would oblige with scenes incorporating them. (Twenty years later they still up to a point work like this.) Ivory noted that he wanted a Maharaja fixing the State cars. He got his odd mechanic (and it is one of those distinctive but almost throwaway moments which mark the film and lend it charm). Geoffrey Kendal and Laura Liddel were prevailed upon to play the Buckinghams themselves, although they took, Ivory has recorded, rather a dim view of the art of film acting; Shashi Kapoor was Sanju, the rich young Indian who

**'Shakespeare Wallah':
Geoffrey Kendal**

'Shakespeare Wallah': Madhur Jaffrey

JI: I could take fifteen minutes out of that film now and they would never be missed – principally entrances and exits. Satyajit Ray suggested cuts while he was composing the music, but I resisted, and when we were watching the film together at the Berlin Film Festival, he again urged me to cut it. I finally did so in New York, but half-heartedly, and without hiring the kind of American editor who would have brought a brisk matter-of-fact professionalism to the task, who needed to shout 'Cut!' at me. I doubt that we could have afforded such an editor, nor am I sure I would have listened to him: pace has often played second fiddle to atmosphere in my films and some-times it should have been the other way round. Best is when pace and atmosphere are the same, as in a film like *Charulata*.

falls for the Buckinghams' restless Indian-born daughter Lizzie, played by the Kendals' own daughter Felicity, in her first film role. The family circle, as it might be called, was completed by additional players from *The Householder*: Madhur Jaffrey as Manjula, a Bombay film star, who has prior claims on Sanju; and Jennifer Kendal as the elderly keeper of Gleneagles.

The appeal of *Shakespeare Wallah*, notably in Britain but also earlier at the 1965 Berlin Film Festival, where it was accepted as the 'Indian' entry following a letter of recommendation from Satyajit Ray and where Madhur Jaffrey took the prize for the best actress, stemmed in part from the fact that it was the first English-language feature film since *The River* to have been set in a believable foursquare India. The tone was elegiac, but the detailing was precise and, on the whole, notably unromantic. It may have rambled* and lacked the conciseness of *The Householder*, which came into distribution in London only after the successful release of *Shakespeare Wallah*, but MIP's technically more ambitious second film was to many Westerners a genuine revelation: the feel of riding in an Indian train; of sleeping outside on string beds – charpoys – under what looked like muslin cheese-covers; the sense of coping with or being defeated by Indian bureaucracy (the finality of a deputy headmaster bouncing a ping-pong ball as he refused to pay for more than one performance by the players); even the sight of Indians caricaturing themselves (though the delectably shrill and cunning Manjula was something more than a carica-ture). The British also found a star in the 18-year-old Felicity Kendal.

Another strength of *Shakespeare Wallah* was its avoidance of the easily caricatured question of India and spiritual enlightenment – a subject which has preoccupied Ruth Jhabvala, was broached in *The Householder*, and is dealt with from different angles in both *The Guru* and *Bombay Talkie*. Merchant Ivory returned to this matter with greater success, because perhaps greater detachment, in *Jane Austen in Manhattan* (1980), in which the guru is an avant-garde theatre director, and *Heat and Dust* (1982), in which the disciple is a fully fleshed-out American. (Ruth Jhabvala's 1970 play *A Call From the East*, which dealt with the arrival in England of the first Indian swamis in the early 1900s, was produced in New York in 1981.) Ivory, however, says that he has never been interested in people trying to enlighten themselves through the East. 'When I have to provide this sort of thing it is against my nature. This has not caused any real conflict, but in my own films I don't want to do too much of it. It is probably a good thing that we never did make the planned film of Ruth's story "How I Became a Holy Mother", because basically I am antipathetic to the whole notion. The European actors depicted in *Shakespeare Wallah* weren't wound up in the mystic wonder of it all.'

Shakespeare Wallah, which cost some $80,000, established Merchant Ivory's presence: it was, Ivory has said, 'our best friend'. The film was chiefly financed from the sale of the world distribution rights of *The Householder* to Columbia

'Shakespeare Wallah': on location at Lucknow

Pictures. This deal, however, was only narrowly concluded. Having passed through London, where it was not taken up by either of the two distribution companies which might have handled what was then regarded as a 'specialised' independent feature, *The Householder* was eventually opened by Columbia Pictures in New York in October 1963. The critical reception was on the whole favourable, but the film, which was being handled in the United States by a Columbia subsidiary, Royal Films, played for only a few weeks. Columbia meanwhile had agreed to pay MIP in India and in rupees, and Merchant had gone to Delhi with the Indian release contract. However, Columbia's India-based representative baulked and payment and the Indian opening were delayed. It was a question of blocked rupees — money earned in India by a foreign company which, theoretically, the Indian government was one day pledged to repatriate.

'I had to stay in Delhi for four or five months and find somebody who understood this whole situation,' Merchant said.* 'We had been given a time limit: at a certain date the government had to have given permission for Columbia to add to its fund of blocked rupees. The man who understood the case was an Additional Secretary at the Ministry of Finance. He had enormous power. He invited to his office the man who represented all the American movie company interests in India and said: "I hear you are trying to get out of the Merchant Ivory *Householder* agreement and if you do that I will see that not a single film of Columbia Pictures or any other American motion picture company is imported into India. Convey it to them." And he shut his file. And the American said: "Oh, I think there's some mistake…".'

Shakespeare Wallah went to the New York Film Festival in September 1965 and was released in the city the following March. No one, however, was interested in taking it in the United States: so Merchant Ivory launched it themselves, hired the Baronet Theatre on Third Avenue and gave the proceeds of the

JI: Meanwhile, I had to stay in New York and try to keep some line of communication open with the people at Columbia Pictures. As the months passed, this became more and more difficult, and the whole thing passed into the hands of expensive lawyers, where it stuck. Expensive for us, of course, not for Columbia, who had their own lawyers. But one day it became unstuck a bit, when the Indian Consul General in New York, Sunil Roy, telephoned Abe Schneider, the President of Columbia, to try on our behalf to find out what was going on, and Schneider did not return his call. Roy then wrote him a polite but indignant letter signing it Minister Extraordinary and Pleni… – whatever it is. Schneider is supposed to have received this letter the same day the MPEA [Motion Picture Export Association of America] representative in India sent Columbia an excited message, about a total embargo on all American films, and that broke the log-jam. A day or so later we were informed by our lawyers that Columbia would release *The Householder* in India after all and pay us our money. I had been invited for a weekend on Long Island and was so overcome with emotion and relief I got sick and couldn't come down to dinner. My hostess had a renowned French chef. I never forgave Columbia for that spoiled evening even when we all shook hands later in their Fifth Avenue offices and were again being called by them 'The Boys'. 'What are you boys going to do next?' they beamed at me. I learned then that the most terrible things can happen to you in movie companies, but they're all part of the game, and if you win a point, they'll win the next one, and so on.

39

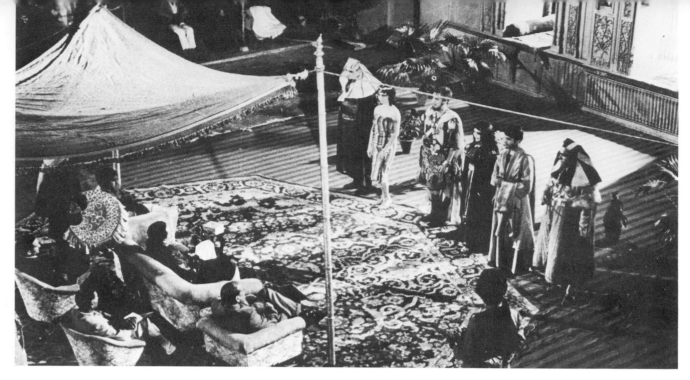

'Shakespeare Wallah': the Maharaja and the players

premiere to UNICEF. 'You believed in the film,' Merchant said, 'and now the film had to provide for you. Now the child had to earn its living. We gambled on the publicity, $20,000. But the film did well and played for about eight weeks. An option had been given to Walter Reade-Sterling, who owned the Baronet as well as a number of other first-run art houses in New York, and who had also gone into distribution. They exercised the option, and Fox bought the film for some overseas territories. *Shakespeare Wallah* started to play all over: but still the exhibitors were slow in coming. We played in Long Island, the West Coast a little later, Washington, Boston. In San Francisco it did very well.' The struggle, however, was only just beginning. 'One always likes to hear about people who are going to get money for you. But something invariably goes wrong: the man who has promised you the stars will not give you a bowl of dust. It is written. You do one thing and you think you have fulfilled something. Surely the next time it will be easier. But it never is.'

p.c–MIP. *p*–IM. *d*–JI. *asst. to p*–Mohamed Shafi. *p. manager*–N. Kabir *asst. d*–Prayag Raaj; R. Shukla. *sc*–RPJ, JI. *ph*–Subrata Mitra. *asst. camera*–Fatik Mazumdar, N. Sarkar. *ed*–Amit Bose; (*asst.*) K.L. Naik. *m*–Satyajit Ray. *choreo*–Sudarshan. *cost*–Jennifer Kendal. *make-up*–Nath Grover. *sd. ed*–Prabhakar Supare. *sd. rec*–Dev Roy. *sd. re-rec*–Mangesh Desai. *p. assistants*–Abbas Khan, Ali Raza. *cast*–Shashi Kapoor (*Sanju*), Geoffrey Kendal (*Tony Buckingham*), Laura Liddel (*Carla*), Felicity Kendal (*Lizzie*), Jim Tytler (*Bobby*), Prayag Raaj (*Sharmaji*), Pincho Kapoor (*Guptaji*), Partap Sharma (*Aslam, the juvenile lead*), Madhur Jaffrey (*Manjula*), Praveen Paul (*Didiji, Manjula's companion*), Utpal Dutt (*the Maharaja*), Hamid Sayani (*the Deputy Headmaster*), Jennifer Bragg [Jennifer Kendal] (*Mrs Bowen*), Marcus Murch (*Dandy in 'The Critic'*), Ismail Merchant (*Theatre Owner*), Sudarshan (*Manjula's Dance Director*). 125 mins (35 mm).

THE GURU

Nana Palsikar, Utpal Dutt

Utpal Dutt, Michael York, Rita Tushingham
Locations: Bombay, Bikaner, Benares
Shooting: December 1967 to April 1968
Premiere: New York, April 1969

After *Shakespeare Wallah* there was a pause of more than two years. In 1966, Ruth Jhabvala completed a script titled *A Lovely World*, a sequel which followed Lizzie, the Felicity Kendal character in *Shakespeare Wallah*, to romance in swinging London, but matters did not develop. Swinging London passed. Meanwhile, in New York, Merchant and Ivory had geared themselves to make an American picture: Lillian Ross was commissioned to adapt her novel *Vertical and Horizontal*. The project, however, faltered protractedly. Paramount had agreed to finance three Merchant Ivory movies, providing suitable subjects could be agreed. They could not. For several years, however, Ivory, who had come to know several leading Indian musicians, including Ravi Shankar and Vilayat Khan, had been contemplating a film about an Indian musician, a maestro, and his devoted but unmusical European disciple.* The idea, with one change, that the disciple became a pop star, seemed to have met its moment: Ravi Shankar had, amid much publicity, become a mentor of the Beatle George Harrison. 'We presented this scheme, *The Guru*, to 20th Century-Fox and they commissioned a screenplay,' Merchant said. 'They'd

JI: All this was based on the real-life relationship of Graeme Vanderstoel, an Australian friend of mine, and Ustad Ali Akbar Khan. If we'd kept it that way, how much better the film might have been. But then, Fox might not have backed it.

41

'The Guru': Rita Tushingham

JI: Satyajit Ray wrote a letter on our behalf to Mrs Gandhi, who reluctantly urged that Dutt be set free. She was reluctant, as a politician, to ask a favour from the government of West Bengal – the arresting authority – who might then turn around and ask *her* for a favour, but she did it. The whole thing was very murky. It turned out that Dutt's arrest had been ordered on the last day an old – a communist – government had been in power, and the new, Congress Party government had not rescinded the order. It didn't help matters that the communists in West Bengal were divided into two fiercely warring factions. It seems that Dutt – an agitator playwright, with his own very popular theatre – had been done in by the rival communist party. If 20th Century-Fox had known about all this, I'm sure they would have considered pulling out, but they merely sent us a mildy anxious telegram or two, by which time Dutt had been returned to us. He said he used the time in jail to practise the sitar for his part in *The Guru*.

liked *Shakespeare Wallah* very much. At that time Fox was actively involved in production in Britain, and this was to be a British production. Ruth, Jim and I went to Bikaner in Rajasthan on a location search and we came to know a lot more musicians. Ruth wrote the screenplay very quickly; I presented it to Fox and within 48 hours we had the go-ahead.'

Matters did not continue so smoothly. 'With *The Guru*,' Merchant said, 'we felt we were moving into a bigger area: more money, two European stars, Michael York and Rita Tushingham, the luxury of an expense account, the hotels taken care of.' 'The people who came out hated India and they didn't get on,' Ruth Jhabvala said. 'Jim was worried and anxious. Nothing went right. The main actor, the guru, Utpal Dutt (the Maharaja in *Shakespeare Wallah*), was arrested on the first day of shooting for being a communist, an agitator, and they had to go through terrible scenes to get him out of jail.* It was as though from the word go some frightful hand of doom was on it. No scene really gets going. They just lie there, heavily. The clothes were all wrong – even for Swinging London. Sometimes what you write just doesn't take off; it doesn't have some inner quality to make it rise. Something's missing. There are some nice scenes. I thought the two wives very good. I liked the music. But that's about all. And some of the settings. I think the Bikaner palace is wonderful and the girl's vision is very good. The intention was that these two young English people were going deeper and deeper into India, until they couldn't stand it any longer. The palace where they end up was the heart of darkness.' Ivory himself has described, in an essay on shooting in the palaces of Royal India, published in 1975 to accompany the script of *Autobiography of a Princess*, some of these misfortunes and the generally poisoned atmosphere of the production. Merchant, ever the optimist and always unwilling to speak ill of his children, has observed that '*The Guru* cost $860,000 but unfortunately, as so often with a major film company, Fox decided not to make the additional investment necessary to promote the film …despite the excellent reviews.' Ivory demurs: 'They weren't that great. People – critics – suggested that we had gone "commercial" …ha!'

The principal problem with *The Guru* is that one of its central characters, Tom Pickle, the naive pop star (Ivory: 'he was supposed to be street wise'), is neither an authentic Ivory nor an authentic Jhabvala character. The guru himself – and even more perhaps the guru's own, ancient, engagingly worldly guru – most definitely is. Tom Pickle, uneasily played by Michael York, is all tiresome vacuity: for all his eagerness to experience India, he seems a curiously incurious visitor. And the trouble is that, unlike the even more vacant Westerners of *The Householder*, from whom he is lineally descended, he holds centre stage. The script treats him with almost the same embarrassment – and in a way rightly so, for he seems to show little awareness of the fact that 'stardom' requires him to behave sometimes as a faintly ridiculous idol – as his guru, the musician, the fastidious Ustad. Their final reconciliation, a garlanded airport parting, is more than a little strained.

What remains of incidental interest is the Ustad's troubles. He has two squabbling wives. The elder (Madhur Jaffrey), having given birth to five daughters in Bombay, calls in a holy woman (Zohra Segal) to cast a malign spell on the younger (Aparna Sen), who is pregnant in Benares with the baby she has confidently been assured – and she has taken occult precautions – will be the longed-for son. (This subject is neatly taken up in MIP's next film *Bombay Talkie*.) The Ustad's weary, perplexed mediation between them registers with greater conviction, with authentic, domestic particularity, than his attempt to sort out Tom Pickle's childlike, essentially self-centred troubles and indecisions. In one scene in particular the two sides of the Ustad's problems are tellingly brought together. Tom and the junior wife are caught innocently waltzing among some rooftop begonias: the Ustad looks like thunder; his wife silently disengages herself and disappears inside; the blank Englishman cannot for the life of him understand what has happened.

The film is flecked with engaging touches: the English girl (Rita Tushingham) being taught how to put on a sari; the entry of the Ustad's party to Benares in great humour; a 'Miss Teen Queen' beauty competition with Merchant presiding at the Chicago Radio; the holy woman pinching the English girl's plump arm and clucking delightedly; a vulgarly materialistic Bombay party at which one of the guests (Leela Naidu), to demonstrate her Western sophistication, quotes, straightfaced, one of Tom Pickle's lyrics back at him – 'Is it always going to be like this? Rainy weather, empty bed, ash in my cuppa tea?' But these, like the punctuating musical sequences played by Vilayat Khan, remain self-contained. In the end we are indifferent to Tom Pickle's fate: he should, we feel, never have come to India; he has been an indifferent tourist.

'The Guru': Aparna Sen, Michael York

p.c–Arcadia Films (for 20th Century-Fox)/MIP. *p*–IM. *d*–JI. *assoc. p*–Muriel Neff, Peter Reilly. *p. controller*–Giancarlo Pettini. *p. manager*–Riaz Hafizka. *location manager*–Rashid Abbasi. *asst. d*–Prayag Raaj, Mohamed Shafi; Wasi Khan; Shama Habibullah. *sc*–RPJ, JI. *ph*–Subrata Mitra. *col*–DeLuxe. *asst. camera*–Fatik Mazumdar, Prajanan Mitra. *ed*–Prabhakar Supare; (*asst.*) K.L. Naik, Humphrey Dixon, Shri Ghate, Chris Crane. *a.d*–Bansi Chandragupta; Didi Contractor. *unit ph*–Douglas Webb. *m*–Ustad Vilayat Khan. *songs*–Tom's Boat Song by Ustad Imrat Hussein Khan, RPJ; 'Where Did You Come From?' by Mark London, Don Black. *cost*–Narender Kocher; (Michael York) Gordon Deighton, (Rita Tushingham) Joanna Tyson, (Leela Naidu) Malabar, Bombay. *make-up*–Tony Delaney, Nath Grover. *sd. ed*–Don Ranasinghe, Brian Blamey. *sd. rec*–Dev Roy, Prabhat Das. *cast*–Michael York (*Tom Pickle*), Saeed Jaffrey (*Murad*), Utpal Dutt (*Ustad Zafar Khan*), Madhur Jaffrey (*Begum Sahiba*), Usha Katrak (*Lady Reporter*), Rita Tushingham (*Jenny*), Fred Ohringer (*Howard*), Nargis Cowasji (*Society Hostess*), Leela Naidu (*Girl at the Party*), Marcus Murch (*Snide Guest*), Zohra Segal (*Mustani*), Aparna Sen (*Ghazala*), Barry Foster (*Chris Todd*), Dorothy Strelsin (*Tourist*), Ismail Merchant (*Compere*), Rafi Ameer (*Arnold D' Mellow*), Soni Aurore (*Teen Queen*), Nana Palsikar (*the Guru's Guru*), Nadira (*Courtesan*), Pincho Kapoor (*Murderer*), Shri Agarwal (*Doctor*), Prayag Raaj (*Classical Singer*). 112 mins. (35 mm).

'The Guru': Zohra Segal, Madhur Jaffrey

'Bombay Talkie': Jennifer Kendal, Shashi Kapoor

Jennifer Kendal at the ashram

BOMBAY TALKIE

Jennifer Kendal, Shashi Kapoor, Zia Mohyeddin, Aparna Sen
Locations: Bombay, Elephanta
Shooting: January to March 1970 and July 1970
Premiere: New York, October 1970

'Bombay Talkie': Aparna Sen

Bombay Talkie germinated in 1968 during the making of *The Guru*. The following year, Ivory and Ruth Jhabvala exchanged letters about it between New York and Delhi. In October Ivory went to India and first saw the complete script. Shooting began in Bombay on 15 January 1970. Ivory had become interested in celebrated foreign women, such as Vivien Leigh, who had come to India and whom he had seen there: the film, set in the Bombay film world, which by this time all three members of the partnership knew well, and which Ruth Jhabvala had written about in her novel, *A Backward Place*, was to be built round such a woman. 'Jim wanted to make her an actress, ' Ruth Jhabvala said, 'but since we had had an actress in *Shakespeare Wallah* we decided to have her a sort of transient novelist. Then we also wanted to reflect the whole trashy world of Indian films, together with the trashy Western imagination.'

Ivory had been deeply impressed by the death of Shashi Kapoor's sister-in-law, Geeta Bali, and he wanted an image of a cremation in the film. 'Geeta Bali, who was a wonderful comedienne, had never been vaccinated, her father was against it,' Ivory said. 'Whenever she went out of India she got the family doctor in Bombay to fake a vaccination certificate. If he'd been less obliging, she'd still be with us. Anyway, she went to shoot in a village in the Punjab where there were cases of smallpox and she came down with it after she returned to Bombay. Evidently her death was swift and terrible. I heard about it in the editing room where we were cutting *Shakespeare Wallah*, and Ismail and I hurried to her house. There was a huge crowd outside; her husband, Shammi Kapoor – Shashi's brother – was also a big star. The funeral procession was about to begin. She could not be carried to the cremation grounds in the usual way, on a litter, but had to be removed in strict quarantine in a Health Department vehicle.

'When we got to the burning ghat, which was by the sea, there was an enormous throng. Some of these were the merely curious, hoping to catch a glimpse of the convocation of movie stars, but most were Geeta Bali's friends and co-workers. Some had come straight from their sets, still in the heavy make-up Indian movie actors wear – or wore then, they've toned it down a bit – and everyone was in white, which is traditional. There were no women, which is also traditional. The pyre was lit exactly as the sun was sinking into the sea, as it touched the horizon. There was the usual squabbling among the pandits – 'It has to be done this way.' 'No, that way ... ' – while the crowd waited for the flames to ignite the ghee poured over the form on the sandalwood logs. I felt there was something of the ancient world in all this, it was like a scene from some great Greek tragedy; the funeral of Alexander, or whatever else leapt to mind. And this is what *Bombay Talkie* came out of – but, of course, when it came time for us to try and set up something on the scale of Geeta Bali's funeral, it wasn't possible to bring it off.'*

A shot of a cremation, as Ivory notes, was in fact taken but not ultimately used. However, *Bombay Talkie* does twice draw on this image. In a long speech the film star Vikram (Shashi Kapoor) explains to the novelist the importance he places on having a son, someone to light his funeral pyre. The speech throws an oblique light on his relationship with his barren wife (Aparna Sen). And later, a funeral procession is used as a dramatic device to halt the flight of the novelist (Jennifer Kendal) and fatefully reunite her with Vikram. However, unlike *The Householder* and *Shakespeare Wallah*, Ruth Jhabvala has said that *Bombay Talkie* was chiefly fashioned not round the idea for a plot but from a string of favourite images: a wrestling match; restaurant life; a desire to put on to the screen the Bombay film stars' fantastic bedrooms. Another motive force was that Merchant Ivory wanted a vehicle for their friends Shashi and Jennifer Kapoor.

Merchant's disillusionment with the inadequate promotion of *The Guru* decided him against going to a major company again and sent him down Wall Street to seek finance for the new film. 'I went to merchant banks, mostly people who had not financed films before,' he said. 'We were not alone in doing

'Bombay Talkie': Shashi Kapoor, Utpal Dutt, in the nightclub

JI: The main trouble – as so often with Indian films – was with the extras. We couldn't get the right kind of crowd. You rarely can. We advertised, but for some reason no one came. Perhaps word went around that the scene was to be the funeral of Vikram, Shashi Kapoor, so everyone knew it would be a waste of time to go – he wouldn't be there. The people who did turn up were all wrong, just a lot of poor kids mostly. We'd set up a very elaborate circular track, so that the camera could move 360 degrees round the mourners, always shooting through the flames of the pyre towards their faces, and towards the hysterical Lucia, defying tradition as usual by insisting on being present. But the mourners, apart from principals and supporting players, were a ragged, inappropriate, and – even worse – thin crowd. There was none of the majestic spectacle of Geeta Bali's last rites. The shot failed and we dropped it. There is a tiny footnote to Indian film history in this failure: one of the extras in that shot, glimpsed through the flames, was Amitabh Bachchan, India's biggest star today.

'Bombay Talkie': Lucia's rivals, Zia Mohyeddin and Shashi Kapoor

JI: It wasn't a spoof at all: we bought a sequence from an abandoned Hindi film, partially shot in Venice. One of its stars, Rajshree, had gone off to California to marry an American and never returned to finish.

this, but we went about it in a different way. If we heard that such-and-such a person was wealthy and interested in films, we would find the right introductions. I would not hesitate. This has always proven fruitful, although ninety per cent of the time nothing concrete has emerged. I think we used fifteen to twenty individuals and organisations for *Bombay Talkie*. The man who came up with most of the money, Joseph Saleh, wanted to buy Merchant Ivory Productions, give us a three-year contract and guaranteed income, which was quite attractive but which luckily fell through. He was an Iraqi Jew who dealt in real estate and carpets and wanted to be in films. Shashi himself put up some of the money, as the distributor, for the Indian rights. This was the beginnings of his own Film-Valas company, which has since gone into production as well as distribution.' The film cost $110,000 and was given a characteristic fillip by Merchant having talked his way into the Taj Mahal, Bombay's leading and most sumptuous hotel, for permission to shoot there.

Apart from the image of the cremation, Ivory had in mind another thread. 'I knew some rich Europeans who lived fashionably, mixed up with rich, Westernised Indians from Juhu Beach, a fancy Bombay suburb, and they too entered into it. I satirised these people in the party scene in *The Guru*, but I had begun to wonder what I could do with them more seriously. The Westerners were there to find gurus or to lead comfortable, very pleasant lives. They collected Indian art objects and had sexual adventures. Or they lived in India because it was warm and money would go a long way. But they were like beach bums. I knew much more about them by the time I did *Bombay Talkie*. I knew much more what kind of people they were. Mind you, I went to their houses often enough, ate their food ... I really wasn't out to make fun of them as such, but at least I was aware of them as a class, a strange group. Lucia Lane, the novelist, came out of these people. Originally she was to have been someone living in India. But the script didn't turn out that way. She came from the West on a quest...'

Unlike *The Guru*, *Bombay Talkie* is closely focused. Its observation of the Bombay film world – from the giant prop typewriter in the opening sequence; the restaurant movie talk (everyone, it seems, has roving, anxious eyes); the spoof of Bombay 'Venice' (as fantastical in its own way as 'Paris' Paramount) with the dubbed couple snaking round each other in the Piazza San Marco in their practised efforts to avoid a kiss but suggest carnality;* the fight scene in the film within a film, Vikram whirling a cow-girl like a mace; the sequence with the plausible, chilling producer of 'pornographic' movies (Utpal Dutt again) – unifies the film and stamps it, despite its conscious element of women's magazine parody and in the end outright melodrama, with lived-in authenticity. The down-at-heel Buckinghams, always short on bookings, lived and worked in a similar, though different, world of 'theatrical' unreality to that of the wealthy Vikram, overburdened by his producer's shooting schedule and what he takes to be the lack of understanding of his unhappy wife. Both are locked into their respective worlds, caught by convention, and both are ultimately unable to escape.

Merchant had reservations about *Bombay Talkie*. 'It seemed to me that, somehow, Jennifer was too wholesome as the much-married author of the lurid *Consenting Adults*. The film lacked that feel of Jacqueline Susann being interviewed on the Johnny Carson Show. Jim liked the kitsch, but in a way his taste was too refined for that kind of crass vulgarity.' He has a point: even Lucia's mild expletives sound somewhat unnatural. However, on another plane, Jennifer Kendal's Lucia, with her unblushing pushiness, her heartless sentimentality and her ability to manipulate her admirers, displays a facility which strikes exactly the right note. In the restaurant, for instance, where the film world gathers for sessions of mutual assassination,* she outlines a breathless plan for a project on which she and Vikram – who allows himself, enjoyably, to be taken in by her – could work. She is as unaware as Indu, greedily eating cakes at the principal's tea party, that she is behaving improperly. Hers is naive babble but it is not the same naive babble as that of the English girl in *The Guru*. It is not that India fails to affect her, but rather that she is a character so shallow that she is able to experience it while her mind is preoccupied by other matters. During her stay with the unaesthetic guru (Pincho Kapoor), she seems forever to be losing her place in the hymn book, having to drop out of the devotional processions to tuck up her sari, finding her mind wandering away to handsome young men pouring water over themselves ... In this sense, Lucia Lane is a reprehensible and not very attractive latter-day colonialist, although it is not in the film-makers' natures to make such a judgment.

'**Bombay Talkie**': Jennifer Kendal, Shashi Kapoor

JI: Just about the worst major scene I ever directed. What is that Greek word – stasis – that means the absence of all animation? When I see those extras sitting there like stones, no one moving or talking or even eating and drinking, and the camera not moving either, and even the Indian chanteuse in her beehive hairdo rooted to the spot where the cameraman, Subrata Mitra, put her, I want to hide under the seat. It could have been such a rich scene – it was written as such – but when we got down to doing it I made the mistake of concentrating too narrowly on the dialogue exchanges and lost all the atmosphere. Believe me, an Indian night club has got plenty of atmosphere. The scene ought at least to have had the impact of Chez Nell in *Quartet*, which moreover was a pastiche-like *reconstruction* of a 1920s Paris night club: one had to imagine it, whereas at Sun 'n' Sands in Juhu, where we shot the scene over several nights, the real, lush thing was all about me and I failed to get it on film. A great, great pity.

p.c–MIP. *p*–IM. *d*–JI. *asst. to p*–Mohan Nadkarni, Asha Seth. *p. controller*–Mohamed Shafi. *p. managers*–Narendra Kumar; (asst.) Abbas Shaiku. *asst. d*–Tom Reeves; Awtar Kaul; Shama Habibullah. *continuity*–Janine Bharucha. *sc*–RPJ, JI. *ph*–Subrata Mitra. *col*–Eastman Colour. *asst. camera*–Adeeb Tandon. *ed*–David Gladwell. *a.d*–A. Ranga Raj. *p. artist/titles*–Tilak Raj. *m*–Shankar Jaikishan. *songs*–Hasrat Jaipuri. *playback singers*–Asha Bhonsle, Kishore Kumar, Mohamed Rafi. *choreo*–Sudarshan Dhir. *cost*–Shaikh Hasan. *make-up*–Nath Grover. *sd. ed*–Prabhakar Supare; (asst.) K.N. Chaven, Manohar Redij. *sd. re-rec*–Narendra Singh. *sd. re-rec*–Manghesh Desai, A.K. Parmar. *adviser*–J.F. Van Der Auwera. *film extract*–Naina. *cast*–Shashi Kapoor (*Vikram*), Jennifer Kendal (*Lucia Lane*), Zia Mohyeddin (*Hari*), Aparna Sen (*Mala*), Utpal Dutt (*Bose*), Nadira (*Anjana Devi, Vikram's confidante*), Pincho Kapoor (*Swamiji*), Helen (*Heroine in Gold*), Usha Iyer (*Cabaret Singer*), Sulochana (*Gopal Ma*), Prayag Raaj (*Director*), Jalal Agha, Anwar Ali and Mohan Nadkarni (*Anjana's Young Men*), Sukhdev and Harbans Darshan (*Men at Bar*), Mirza Musharaff (*Fan*), Soni Aurore (*Heroine in Red*), Peter Howard, Angelika Saleh, Nicholas Lear, Tom Reeves and David Gladwell (*Ashram Inmates*), Iftekhar (*Vizarat Khan*), Kamala Mehra (*Operator*), Datta Ram (*Playback Singer*), Mohan Dingra (*Jeweller*), Saudagar Singh and Vasant Singh (*Wrestlers*), Avadh N. Singh (*Referee*), Shama Hussein and Indu Lele (*Two Ladies*), Louis de Souza (*Louis the Servant*), Ismail Merchant (*Fate Machine Producer*). 105 mins. (35 mm).

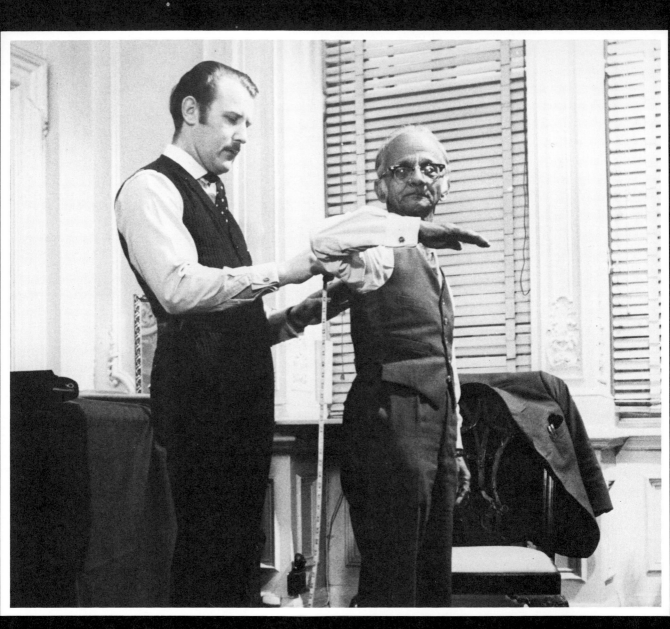

Nirad Chaudhuri and his tailor

Chapter Three

RISE AND FALL

ADVENTURES OF A BROWN MAN IN SEARCH OF CIVILISATION

Nirad Chaudhuri
Locations: Oxford, Chiswick (London)
Shooting: October 1970
Premiere: BBC 2 (UK), April 1972

Bombay Talkie was completed in August 1970, and the company then went to London. They were joined by George Trow, who had first met Merchant at a party given in New York in 1967 by Air India to promote 'paper saris', a fad which did not ultimately catch on. Trow had been covering the occasion for the *New Yorker*'s 'Talk of the Town' column. He and Merchant had kept up, and he was now, at Ivory's suggestion, developing a script, *Stephen's Story*. This was to centre on the experiences of one of Ivory's friends, a fledgling art historian, Stephen Scher, who, while getting his Master's degree at New York University, had worked as an unpaid auxiliary policeman. Once a week he patrolled New York's Central Park on horseback. In the late 1950s, this was on the whole regarded as a romantic rather than a hazardous occupation.

'I had by that time lived for nearly ten years in New York,' Ivory said, 'and I had other notions about life in the city, which I thought might be combined with the idea of the auxiliary policeman. However, being an original writer, George Trow found it very difficult to make something of someone else's idea. He produced an extraordinary fantasy, which was not at all what I had in mind. He didn't really like what he was doing, but he did it seriously. It was, I believe, one of those things that serious writers half-heartedly do, out of which good ideas come for other work, and there are strains of *Stephen's Story*, which

'Adventures of a Brown Man': Mr and Mrs Chaudhuri

was never made, in our next feature, *Savages*, which Trow wrote with Michael O'Donoghue. I didn't at the time realise I was about to go into something quite as fantastic as *Savages*. I tended then, and this is still usually true, to be quite naturalistic, or what I imagine to be naturalistic, and didn't favour a very far-out style of storytelling.'

Merchant, meanwhile, had concluded a swift co-production deal with BBC TV to make a documentary in Oxford on the visiting Indian polymath Nirad Chaudhuri, the author of, among many other works, *The Autobiography of an Unknown Indian* and *The Continent of Circe*. Chaudhuri was in England in pursuit of his researches into the life of the Sanskrit scholar Max Müller. Merchant and Ivory had met Chaudhuri in India and were thus well placed when the BBC's India correspondent proposed the idea of a film about him to the BBC. Ivory was exhausted after *Bombay Talkie*, but was prevailed upon to direct ('I decided that if we were not going to do it now,' Merchant said, 'it would never be done').

'I was not so much exhausted by *Bombay Talkie*,' Ivory said, 'as by its aftermath. Once the film was completed we still had to get a good answer print out of the lab in Bombay. I stayed on to help oversee this with Subrata Mitra. It was the monsoon season and we were living in a perpetual deluge, but for some reason the lab never seemed to have any water, or was it the right kind of water? Anyway, it took weeks to print the film to Mitra's standards. Then the great furore arose while I was still there over *Phantom India* – how Louis Malle had denigrated India and so on, with the consequent expulsion of the BBC and new, strict provisions imposed, still in force, about film-making by foreigners. I was terrified that the Government of India would deny *Bombay Talkie* an export licence, and much given generally to all sorts of other paranoias.'

The shooting schedule was four days, the budget £10,000. George Trow, now 'family', was roped in as a performer, and Walter Lassally, who was henceforth to become Merchant Ivory's favoured director of photography, was engaged as cameraman. *Adventures of a Brown Man in Search of Civilisation* was shot, in Merchant's words, from the hip. Ivory believes that television – public television in the United States and television generally in Britain – has a greater tolerance than the cinema for the 'literary', and the Shavian echo in the title, as well as the small-scale, and very literary, eccentricity of the subject, marks this off as a (serious) television enterprise. Generally, Ivory makes no distinction between the style and content of MIP's film and television work: *Adventures of a Brown Man* is, perhaps, the single exception.* 'The title,' Ivory said, 'in fact comes from one of the chapter titles of Chaudhuri's second book, *Passage to England*, which is about a colonial, Chaudhuri, arriving for the first time in the capital of the Empire, and is full of amusing *pensées* on the complicated Anglo-Indian relationship.'

Set-ups – an incongruous dinner (that MIP trademark), a pilgrimage to a graveyard (another one), a visit to a tailor who opens up to reminisce about

JI: Not true, actually. I *do* make a distinction – both in subject matter and in treatment. Some ideas, very interesting in themselves and worth doing, would not make very good feature films. It's a matter of scale, including the scale of the idea. Television audiences (I mean, those used to watching Public Television in the US and British television) will accept 'difficult', i.e. taxing or unpleasant, subject matter in a way that audiences for entertainment films will not. You can, for instance, have quite a lot of talking heads on serious television; people accept it, even feel cheated if they don't get it. But you can't do that too often in a theatrical feature. On television your images need to be simpler, more graphic, to be effective. Uncluttered. In a long shot on the big screen, however, your eye can wander about and pick out much that is lost on television screens. You can flood the big screen with detail, if you're good at that, or create epic action sequences with hundreds of extras, but it all gets reduced on television, in every sense. Most directors who work in both mediums know this, and plan accordingly. It's one's *enthusiasm* that must not get reduced. In that way, no, we do not generally make a distinction.

Tagore – were arranged and a delighted Chaudhuri was allowed to extemporise, wittily and indefatigably. Chaudhuri was a powerful antidote to the real-life equivalents of Lucia Lane, the Hollywood novelist of *Bombay Talkie*, the incurious Westerner baffled and annoyed by Indian customs. Chaudhuri, an intellectual gadfly in Delhi, found himself entirely at home in Oxford. He behaved correctly with his tailor, that sign that he was both a 'gentleman' and a citizen of the world. (Western women in Merchant Ivory films are, it seems, always having to be instructed in how to wear a sari.) At the dinner party, Chaudhuri even chose, impishly, to denigrate what he took to be the jangle of Indian music and to praise the subtleties of Western symphonic music. His silent wife looked on beatifically (though Ivory judges her look more sceptical than beatific). He gave the impression, rightly no doubt, that he knew more about Western culture than his hosts. The irony did not escape the film-makers.

Ivory: 'I was not so much exhausted by "Bombay Talkie" as by its aftermath...' The cast and crew of 'Bombay Talkie' on Ivory's favourite set, the giant typewriter. Ismail Merchant and cameraman Subrata Mitra emulate Helen and Shashi Kapoor (centre top)

p.c–MIP. *p*–IM. *d*–JI. *p. assoc*–Anthony Korner. *sc*–JI. *ph*–Walter Lassally. In colour. *ed*–Kent McKinney. *sd*–Peter Sutton, Peter Rann. *p. assistant*–Richard Macrory. *narrator*–Barry Foster. *with*–Nirad C. Chaudhuri. 54 mins. (16mm).

The revered croquet ball

SAVAGES

Louis Stadlen, Anne Francine, Thayer David ... and cast
Locations: Scarborough (New York), Richmond Great Park (London)
Shooting: May to June 1971, June 1972
Premiere: Cannes Film Festival, May 1972

**'Savages': Kathleen Widdoes,
Christopher Pennock**

In New York, Ivory continued to work on *Stephen's Story*, although by now he had thoroughly lost interest in the project. 'One day in my apartment,' he said, 'while trying to revise the script, George and I began to talk about the possibility of making *Savages*.' It was to be like *The Exterminating Angel*, except that it would show the rise of civilisation as well as its fall. Ivory already had in mind the house where the rise and fall would occur: Beechwood, an incongruous mixture of American architectural styles from the Revolution on, owned by the Vanderlip family, and situated on the Hudson River near Scarborough, New York. Joseph Saleh liked the idea for the new film, despite the fact that the opening of *Bombay Talkie* had not been auspicious. Over dinner, it was rashly proposed that the movie could be made for as little as $10,000, with Merchant Ivory themselves finding costumes in thrift shops. Saleh agreed to finance the project, although it rapidly became apparent that the elaborate costumes of the Mud People, designed by Anthony Korner, and the hire of the vintage motorcar, a 1930 Pierce-Arrow, which the Savages come upon as the first magnificent, useless sign of civilisation (a perfectly preserved palace in the middle of nowhere), would alone cost that sum.*

Having in Ivory's word 'concocted' a treatment, something which Ruth Jhabvala never does, and realising that matters were serious when money was proposed, George Trow and Michael O'Donoghue got down to writing a script. 'Michael O'Donoghue,' Ivory said, 'who subsequently worked for the *National Lampoon* and is now a highly paid writer for NBC's *Saturday Night Live*, was then a penniless writer living in SoHo – which hadn't become fashionable yet – and could barely makes ends meet.' The idea for the opening, the croquet ball which comes sailing into the forest, luring the Mud People by its perfect, mysterious, spherical shape towards a chimerical civilisation, was O'Donoghue's: and it was his particular task to supply the pastiche monologues – poetically meaningful or poetically meaningless – which punctuate the action. Filming started in May with a non-union crew and a cast chiefly composed of Broadway and off-Broadway actors – Thayer David, Salome Jens, Louis Stadlen, Kathleen Widdoes, Sam Waterston – who were given a dispensation by the Screen Actors' Guild owing to the production's low budget. Ivory had noted Anne Francine, who here plays the priestess transformed to Carlotta, the society hostess, in Fellini's *Juliet of the Spirits*. 'I always thought,' he said, 'that one day I would make a film which would require a woman like that, who spoke with that kind of accent, a good Philadelphia accent.'

Money was tight, and, to raise their spirits, Merchant inaugurated his sometime practice of cooking the company lavish Friday evening meals after the screening of the rushes. 'Only two-thirds of the script was completed when we started shooting, and so we were compelled up to a point to shoot the treatment,' Ivory said. 'The script peters out at about the moment that the assembled characters listen to the broadcast of the sinking ship. The rest was eventually written. But by then George Trow had become involved in something else and was preparing to go down to Mississippi on another writing assignment. He would sit in the motel where we were staying and bat out pages, which would then come to us on set, but his mind was really down South. Once or twice he would come on set while we were shooting and wouldn't like the way actors were delivering lines. I'd be giving direction and he would say, "It can't be like that, it must be like this…" Somewhat confusing for the actors. This aside, I did work very closely with George. Though not in the way I work with Ruth. She is continuously writing throughout the production, if she feels that something is going wrong or a character is not coming out, or if an actor can't handle a role, or if another is wonderfully good and needs more role. George's reaction – and Michael's too, though not so much Michael, because he is more of a man of the world and because he became intrigued – was that he wanted to get away. It was George's first movie, and for him to have to go on set and hear his lines being, as he believed, ruined

'Savages': Oriental hokum

JI: Though we later had an awful falling-out with Joe Saleh, since repaired, I must say that he was one of the most indulgent of our financiers and ought to be given credit for a largeness of spirit – not to mention pocketbook – that you don't often find in our kind of independent film financing. He liked us, liked our earlier films, and backed *Bombay Talkie* solely on that basis, though he was apprehensive about its commercial chances. When those fears were unfortunately confirmed, instead of kicking us out, he immediately wanted to get going on a new project again, rather like Ismail does. We told him the 'story' of *Savages* over dinner in about five minutes, and by the end of the meal we had his commitment – and when the budget ended up being perhaps thirty times greater, he was *still* enthusiastic.

'Savages': Anne Francine

'Savages': Asha Puthli

was terribly distressing. Though I remember that Ruth was once similarly distressed, during *The Guru*. She came to Bikaner and watched the scene with the guru's guru, in which he's sitting up in bed and telling the disciple-guru how fat he has become from luxurious living and consorting with foreigners. It was originally a much longer scene, but the old actor could not remember his lines and Ruth didn't like the way he was saying the ones he could remember. She sat down and rewrote the scene there and then. And we shot that the next day. She spoke right out, though not in front of the actor.'

In the course of an article on *Savages* in the Autumn 1971 issue of *Sight and Sound*, Ivory has this to say about his location: 'Just as India by virtue of its overwhelming presence was a character – in fact, a central character – of both *Shakespeare Wallah* and *The Guru*, Beechwood House similarly imposed itself upon everything, from the actual scene-by-scene construction of the film to the choice of costumes and props. The rooms of the house, like those in the houses of many American millionaires, were decorated in different styles – pseudo Renaissance, pseudo Adam, French 18th century, Japanese. The episodes which were set in those rooms corresponded to a time in the savages' "history" and tended to be used only once, except for rooms of passage – stairs, hallways, etc. – which appear again and again.

'Though much picked over by members of the Vanderlip family, the furniture, objects, pictures, etc. were largely intact, and closets and attics were full of the clothes and possessions of several generations. All this was at our disposal, including an extraordinary set of Chinese robes which came in handy when the savages reach the stage of degeneracy in which they go in for exotic hokum and dope-taking. The house was a kind of time capsule, sealed at the end of the 30s by the Second World War, when the Vanderlip men went into the services and the staff left – one imagines – for the war plants. Nothing was ever changed after that, and so we put our savages into the clothes of that decade, which also removed them from a too-familiar present with its own associations.'

'Apart from Beechwood itself,' Ivory said, 'I was influenced in other ways. While I was cutting *Adventures of a Brown Man*, down in an editing room in Chelsea, New York, the Elgin Theater (since closed) was having a revival of all the D. W. Griffith films, and after work I'd walk a couple of blocks south and go in there. The Griffith film that somehow influenced me the most was *Way Down East*, particularly the satirical scenes set in a fancy New York town house, in which a fashionable party is going on (circa 1920), into which Lillian Gish is introduced. The hostess and her sneering friends, in gowns with little trains like the backs of some species of beetle, wearing headdresses with – I seem to remember antenna-like projections, resembled predatory insects as they darted this side and that on thin, pointed feet. Carlotta in *Savages* is a descendant of Griffith's heartless, angular, upper-class hostess.

'Then I was also influenced by *Fellini Satyricon*. Most films about Ancient Rome have been a succession of set-pieces which fail completely to convey any atmosphere that you can believe in, and particularly anything which you might call a moral atmosphere. They are antiseptic: the marble gleams, the lions in the arena snarl, but you remain unconvinced. Fellini threw all that kind of detail overboard and instead projected – at least for me – a feeling of what Rome must have been like when all the underpinnings of law and order were collapsing and society no longer had any standards of behaviour beyond conspicuous gratification. His best sequences – like the mystic marriage aboard the cube-galleon on the storm-tossed sea, or the kidnap of the albino child-deity who is trundled around in a wheelbarrow until he/she/it dies – have a weird power that gives you the shivers and are quite unforgettable. They make you feel, yes, that really must have been the way it was then.'

Savages, with which Ivory remains pleased,* with the small proviso that he regrets having omitted his civilisation's Golden Age, is a film of abstract pleasures. And being so, it runs the risk of seeming merely whimsical. It is, however, both nonsensical and precise: the half-naked Mud People who emerge from their friendly New York wood with their elaborate, anthropologically correct* masks behave rather like the primitives in *Brother Jasper*, the pastiche silent film comedy around which MIP's next feature, *The Wild Party*, revolves; but the unseen narrator, who expatiates on their progress in unsubtitled German (he's actually quoting Heine and Schiller), appears to take their behaviour, or his own perception of it, with the utmost seriousness. The savages, who have been interrupted in the middle of a human sacrifice, adhere to a strict hierarchy. As they cautiously creep – fingering a statue, licking a family portrait – into the mansion from whose lawns the croquet ball has come, they rapidly shed their loin-cloths and immense masks and exchange them for only slightly less preposterous garments and manners. The hierarchy, however, remains immutable. The bully remains the bully, the limp young man the limp young man, the servant the servant.

That the following always witty and sometimes arch series of anecdotal vignettes (behaviour under a magnifying glass) remains beguiling, given that the antagonists do not actually do anything, is partly because Ivory and his director of photography, Walter Lassally, so neatly capture the tone of an idyllic, vacant, country weekend. It seems, in this context, perfectly natural for an elderly couple to be caught idly swinging on an elaborate garden chair while peeling a cabbage; for the younger members of the party, out of boredom or perhaps frustration at being trapped by their more powerful elders, to divert themselves by trapping bees and sizzling them under a magnifying glass. To attempt an interpretation of these goings-on – of the meaning, for instance, of the elaborate cut-and-thrust of the climactic dinner which marks the apogee of civilisation and which is interrupted by the croquet ball rolling

JI: Well, pretty pleased. There's a lot of the 'decadent' goings-on which could have been better; those sequences are a little slapdash, or maybe too tenuous to be dramatic. I like the dope-taking with the Oriental hocus-pocus, and I like the submerged corpse in the swimming pool being robbed by the Boy-of-Good-Family. I like the poet-songwriter, Julian Branch, turning his back on it all and, like a hermit of the Dark Ages, locking himself up in a tower and going in for solitary pursuits. But after 'Steppin' on the Spaniel', the film is to my mind very patchy – all the way up to the point the new savages break out of the cellar and take flight a few minutes before the end, when it all comes together again and which I like very much.

JI: Our Mud People were based on the Mudmen of New Guinea. We saw pictures of them in a magazine advertisement for Canadian Club whisky: one of those completely straight-faced ads where white-skinned sahibs wearing pith helmets are seen having adventures in some dangerous place in the bush. Later, back at their camp, they break out a bottle of their favourite whisky and sit around talking about their exciting day.

purposefully across the floor, luring the savages back to the wood – is in a sense to miss the point: the surface show is the point, the display of manners is meant to be as impermanent as the Mud People's make-up. And yet there is a real world of sorts outside this 30s weekend party: we hear that an ocean liner sinks off the Irish coast; that a railroad (and the Vanderlips, the collectors of all this finery, were Midwesterners who made their money from the railroads) has destroyed a primitive culture. The regretful, half-melancholic echoes which reverberated in *Shakespeare Wallah* of times past refusing wholly to disappear and of a distant, almost unknowable present, reverberate in *Savages* too.

Savages is an absurdist comedy, and as in the best absurdist comedy its *non sequiturs* rebound with echoes. Penelope, the High-Strung Girl (in the opening titles each character is given his or her governing trait), tells a story about a painter, a model of whose Grecian villa is in Carlotta's library. O'Donoghue's monologue is a perfectly embroidered dinner-table story, flecked with detail and atmosphere. One is sucked into it, believes in it for similar reasons that one believes in 'The Walrus and the Carpenter'. Each one of the incidents in *Savages* – one of the women girlishly showing another her breasts; the Bully, Nürder, heartlessly putting down an idealistic young man at the dinner table; a sparkling dance number, 'Steppin' on the Spaniel', followed by a wincingly inadequate rendition of 'We're all out for good old number one' ('Is it possible that the talent of our friend Julian has been overrated?' the hostess asks about her latest protégé); a discussion on the removal of facial hair; a game of charades played in a coal cellar – is complete in itself. Nothing quite comes together, achieves a climax. One character is drowned, another hangs herself. But as at a weekend party, no one except the indifferent hostess is actually responsible; the characters are caught in a dead time, there is really no reason to do anything – to bring forward the dawn of the Golden Age, that perhaps faintly undramatic period which Ivory and his scriptwriters omitted.*

The distribution fate of *Savages*, which eventually cost $300,000, is an object lesson. In the United States the film just missed being taken by the Cinema 5 group of New York. Had this happened, Ivory believes, it would have had the requisite send-off, been part of the right library. Which is not to say that it would have made a fortune: a goal that MIP have never actively sought. As it was, the company was again compelled to turn distributor. They four-walled the Baronet in New York in June 1972, and Joseph Saleh paid for the newspaper advertising. Sub-distributors slowly gathered. 'It played for six weeks in New York and then vanished,' Ivory said. 'It played for a long time in Boston and up and down California and in college towns. There were seven prints. They disappeared just like that. From time to time, you hear that someone saw *Savages* on TV or that someone else saw it somewhere in California or Michigan. Those were all the prints that people made off with. As a final blow the negative seemed to be lost. Joe Saleh had taken it out of the

JI: I wanted to call the film *Trow and O'Donoghue's Ancient History* – exactly like some musty old text-book – but was overruled. Well, in our text-book the film, each scene was planned as a metaphor for an episode in the rise and fall of civilisation. If the American viewers had only looked at it with that in mind, it would have made more sense to them and been more enjoyable. For instance, when the party guests put on Oriental robes and start chanting and taking drugs, one might imagine Rome at the time the Eastern mystery cults became fashionable. One could even think of today. Or, when the well brought-up young man robs a body, that represents not only the epitome of bad manners, but also the time of tomb-robbing, that creepy period in disintegrating societies. When the sensitive girl tells her story about the painter, Chatfield, we have arrived at the Flowering of Literature – and it's sickening after a few, brief moments. Such were the conceits of our dramatic structure. All this presupposes a rudimentary feeling for history. Now, however, I know that if you stopped fifty people on Fifth Avenue and asked them: 'Who was Cleopatra? When did she live?' or even 'What is Abraham Lincoln remembered for?' no more than five could tell you, and maybe not even that many.

laboratory and it had ended up in the basement of one of his apartment houses. Ismail found it, in the end, mercifully undamaged...'

'Savages': the dinner party

Savages appealed to a European sensibility. It was warmly received at both the 1972 Cannes and London Festivals and was subsequently taken into distribution in Britain by Hemdale. It opened in the United States without, however, the cachet of a European art house reputation. Unlike *The Guru*, an unconventional but at least identifiable studio picture, *Savages* was a commercial – if off-beat commercial – film which in a sense came out of nowhere. 'To think that those boys who made those nice Indian films could make this sophomoric thing,' Ivory said. 'That was the general tone of the American criticism, although the *New York Times* and the *New Yorker* both liked it.' *Savages* was a parodic (as well as an absurdist) comedy, but a *New Yorker*-ish parody. It was hardly parodic or sophomoric in the sense that more recent money-spinning campus comedies have been. Ivory was poking fun at Scott Fitzgerald not Harold Lloyd. His subject was essentially patrician.

---

p.c–Angelika Films in association with MIP. *exec. p*–Joseph J. M. Saleh. *p*–IM. *d*–JI. *assoc. p*–Anthony Korner. *p. manager*–Jean-Luc Botbol. *asst. d*–Jeffrey Jacobs, Stephen Varble, Nathaniel Tripp, Serge Nivelle. *sc*–George Swift Trow, Michael O'Donoghue. Based on an idea by JI. *continuity*–Janet Kern. *ph*–Walter Lassally. In colour. *asst. camera*–Jeffrey Bolger, Robert Kenner. *ed*–Kent McKinney; (asst.) Mary Brown. *a.d*–James D. Rule, Jack Wright; (asst.) Susan Middeleer. *illustration and titles*–Charles E. White III. *lettering and title design*–Michael Doret; (asst.) Edward Robbins. *m*–Joe Raposo. *musicians*–Joe Raposo (*piano*), Jim Mitchell (*guitar and banjo*), Bob Cranshaw (*bass*), David Nadieu (*solo violin*), Alan Shulman (*solo cello*), Danny Epstein, Ed Shaughnessy (*percussion*), Walter Kane, Don Ashworth (*woodwind*). *song*–'Savages' by Michael O'Donoghue, George Swift Trow, sung by Bobby Short. *choreo*–('Steppin' on the Spaniel') Patricia Birch. *cost*–(design) Susan Schlossman, Joan Hanfling, (wardrobe) Janice Moore. *make-up*–Gloria Natale. *hairstyles*–Martin Downey. *sd*–Gary Alper; (asst.) John Flynn. *sd. re-rec*–Jack Cooley. *p. assistants*–Frank Di Bari, Howard Goodman, Roger Moorey, Mohan Nadkarni, S. Ruth Gringras, Rick Raphael, Dustin Smith, Robin Schwartz, Emanuel Olivencia, Alice Marsh. *narrators*–Lilly Lessing, Claus Jurgen. *cast*–Louis Stadlen (*Julian Branch, a Songwriter*), Anne Francine (*Carlotta, a Hostess*), Thayer David (*Otto Nürder, a Capitalist*), Susie Blakely (*Cecily, a Debutante*), Russ Thacker (*Andrew, an Eligible Young Man*), Salome Jens (*Mrs Emily Penning, a Woman in Disgrace*), Margaret Brewster (*Lady Cora*), Neil Fitzgerald (*Sir Harry*), Eva Saleh (*Zia, the Child*), Ultra Violet (*Iliona, a Decadent*), Asha Puthli (*Asha, the Forest Girl*), Martin Kove (*Archie, a Bully*), Kathleen Widdoes (*Leslie*), Christopher Pennock (*Hester*), Sam Waterston (*James, the Limping Man*), Paulita Sedgwick (*Penelope, a High-Strung Girl*). 106 mins. (35mm).

'The Wild Party'

Helen, Queen of the Nautch Girls (left)

HELEN
QUEEN OF THE NAUTCH GIRLS

Helen
Location: Bombay
Shooting: January 1971
Premiere: Museum of Modern Art, New York City, March 1973

That Merchant Ivory's attitude to the truly 'popular', or at least to one quirky aspect of it, was not in fact disdain but half-spellbound, half-aghast curiosity was proven – and more emphatically, perhaps, than in *Bombay Talkie* – by a documentary shot and compiled by Merchant and Anthony Korner in 1973. *Helen, Queen of the Nautch Girls* contrasted the real-life (as told to Korner) and the celluloid persona (as exemplified in a number of clips) of the Anglo-Indian star Helen. She had by that time, as the opening title of the film, a mellifluous press handout, announced, sung and danced her way through 500 Hindi movies. She had also appeared on the giant typewriter in *Bombay Talkie*. The commentary which Ivory wrote offered a sociological-cum-artistic gloss, though not one that aped the Germanic solemnity of *Savages'* mock-commentary. He pointed out that cities and foreign parts, in which the on-screen Helen was often to be found, held a particular fascination for Indian moviegoers, ninety per cent of whom lived in small villages.

The film, however, is not primarily the explanation of a phenomenon. Its tone is disinterested. The frenzied vulgarity – to Western middle-class eyes – of Helen's performance, the gaudiness of the sets on which she cavorts, the clothes she wears (all of which one might be tempted to view as the trappings of a primitive cinema), are offset by the presence of Helen herself, straight-forward, unaffected, hard-working. She is concerned with professionalism, that her films have a consistent point of view, that her eyes, more than anything, hold the spectator's attention. When she retires in three or four years, she would like to open a modest boutique in Bombay's then still uncompleted Sheraton Hotel. She would call it, perhaps, 'Something Nice and Groovy'. Like Nirad Chaudhuri, Helen might have been viewed from an incredulous Western standpoint, turned into a figure of fun. But the film steps back, gives her the floor. One does not laugh at her aspirations, even now, when the name of her prospective shop seems an echo from some distant past – as unreal as Tom Pickle himself. The caged black man, seen in one of the clips, driven wild by Helen's unavailability in a nightclub in some Never Never Delhi or Bombay, bursts with life – even if 'vulgar', melodramatic life. Both Helen and Chaudhuri justify themselves by their own lights: driven, energetic individuals, prospering against the odds in, on the whole, a dull-witted world.

---

p.c–MIP. *p*–IM. *d*–Anthony Korner. *sc*–JI. Parts in colour. *addit. ph*–R. M. Rao, Anwar Siraj. *ed*–Andrew Page. *narrator*–Anthony Korner. film extracts–*Prince, Jahan Piyar Milay, Gumnam,* *Nadan, Sachhai, Intequam, Caravan, Howrah Bridge, Sinbad Alladin Alibaba, Bombay Talkie.* *with*–Helen. 31 mins. (16mm).

The mad boy

MAHATMA AND THE MAD BOY

Sajid Khan
Location: Juhu Beach (Bombay)
Shooting: July to August 1972
Premiere: London, March 1974

In the course of a rather spiky interview with two Indian reporters published in the *Hindustan Times* (25 April 1971), James Ivory was asked: 'Do you think a foreigner can really depict our Indian ways truthfully?' 'I think,' he replied, 'that you make too much of "our Indian ways". Indians seem to imagine that they're absolutely unique among mankind, that their every action, their every thought and word, are very special, really unfathomable. But when one is here for a while, the mystification of "our Indian ways" tends to disappear. A foreigner comes gradually to think that, after all, Indians aren't all that different. Indians want the same things as everybody else. They do share what I guess you could call, for want of anything better, a common humanity. Their behaviour, though it may differ in its details a great deal from what we know in the West, is usually motivated by the same things here as in America or Europe or anywhere else.

'You don't have to make a deep study of a lot of what you see in India to know how and where it all fits in, not after ten years at any rate. Now, what I've personally observed has admittedly been pretty much restricted to the urban middle class and I know that's not all of India, or even very much of it. We just present the little bit we know, or think we know, and it's an outsider's point of view. We don't claim to present India as an Indian can and should. What you get in our films is a foreign viewpoint always. We don't try to be Indian. That would be futile.'

An oblique light is thrown on this statement of principle by the second short subject made by Merchant Ivory Productions (but without Ivory) in 1973: *Mahatma and the Mad Boy*. The action covers a day on Bombay's Juhu Beach, some of whose wealthy inhabitants Ivory satirised in *Bombay Talkie*. *Mahatma*, which was filmed by Subrata Mitra, in lyrical mood, and produced and directed by Ismail Merchant, also satirises these wealthy Westernised Indians (and a group of pious Gandhi-ites), but ostensibly from the point of view of a destitute Indian teenager, the 'mad boy', who with the help of his companion monkey begs and steals a living and converses, philosophically, with a statue of an attentive Mahatma Gandhi. The film, which cost some $30,000, was shot in five days; and the music, by Suman Raj and Ram Narayan, which distinctively marks its tone, was recorded in a single three-hour session on the last day of shooting. 'We went straight from the location to the recording studio,' Merchant said. 'Vivaldi's Four Seasons was the musicians' inspiration.'

Although the film is drawn from an Indian story, by Tanveer Farooqi, is made by Indians (though the boy speaks notably idiomatic English), and is centred on a local Indian phenomenon, the Gandhi following to which a visiting government Minister gives a comic, diplomatic moment of his time, *Mahatma* is not really concerned with 'our Indian ways'. Its tone is distantly regretful, but not quite in the couched James Ivory manner; its meaning, like the character of its director, is more straightforward – a plump lady anoints herself with lotion, the monkey scampers off with the bottle; the boy anoints the monkey's face, the monkey licks up the lotion. Considering *Mahatma and the Mad Boy* in retrospect, it appears a particularly appropriate and telling film for Merchant to have made (and Ivory has said that his producer, who rarely stops working, makes his own films privately, as a form of relaxation.) The plot is about a Bombay boy who lives by his wits and is denied even the crumbs from the rich man's table. One can imagine Ismail Merchant, as he hurries through the financial districts of the world's capital cities, casting his thoughts back to the mad boy.

---

p.c–MIP. *p/d*–IM. *sc/story*–Tanveer Farooqi. *ph*–Subrata Mitra. In colour. *asst. camera*–Abid Tandon. *ed*–Andrew Page. *a.d*–Bansi Chandragupta. *m*–Suman Raj. *sarangi player*–Ram Narayan. *make-up*–Ragunath Parwar. *sd*–Madan Prakash. *sd. re-rec*–Peter Rann. *cast*–Sajid Khan (*the Mad Boy*), Sulochana (*the Woman Feeding a Dog*), Shastri (*the Gandhi-ite Speaker*), the people of Juhu Beach, Bombay. 27 mins. (16mm).

Madhur Jaffrey

AUTOBIOGRAPHY OF A PRINCESS

Madhur Jaffrey, James Mason
Location: Kensington (London), Rajasthan
Shooting: January 1971, April 1973 (Rajasthan), March 1974 (Kensington)
Premiere: New York Film Festival, October 1975

Merchant Ivory Productions made two features in 1974. One was their least trouble-free, the other their most problematic. The first, *Autobiography of a Princess*, which was produced for $70,000 and filmed in five days in a flat in Kensington, West London, had been conceived a year earlier by Ivory. During 1971-3, Merchant and Anthony Korner had been assembling material for an unspecified documentary: interviews with the descendants of Royal India and archival footage, the princes' home movies from the 20s to the 40s, which for the most part had been left to decay in India's increasingly disused palaces. Knocked out by the intense April heat of Jodhpur, where he and Ruth Jhabvala had gone in company with their colleagues, Ivory was struck by a notion. 'I began to think of what Bai-ji, the Jodhpur princess, had told us,' he wrote in the preface to the published script of *Autobiography*, 'about her life here, about going to school in Switzerland and then coming back to Jodhpur, and how everybody had tried to force her into purdah. Suddenly I thought of the actress Madhur Jaffrey: what a princess she would make!'

'Ismail is really the first touchstone,' Ruth Jhabvala said. 'If he does not like an idea Jim proposes, he's not going to go ahead with it. We have really to convince him it's something we like. Then he says, yes, but he'd like this better or that better, or why can't we do this or that. And then only when he's in the mood will he go out and get the money, which is the hardest thing of all. We have really to charge him up.' (With *Autobiography*, Merchant persuaded Volkswagen USA, who had never previously invested in film production, to promise $34,000 which was to be matched by an investment from the publishers Harper & Row. The film was to be produced for WNET/13 in New York and needed underwriting, but when it turned out that Harper & Row were about to publish a book on India and that their financing *Autobiography* might be construed as advertising, WNET objected. Volkswagen were persuaded to advance a further $34,000 and became the sole underwriters.) 'Is Ismail hard to please?' Ruth Jhabvala asked. 'Some things he doesn't like at all, and says no, I don't want to have anything to do with it, and so we just don't say any more. Now with *Autobiography of a Princess* he started the whole thing himself by setting out to make a documentary and taking us with him.'

Autobiography remains Ruth Jhabvala's favourite among her films. It was filmed as written with only one line subsequently added. 'Jim wanted the story of a princess, her autobiography,' Ruth Jhabvala said. 'She was to tell her own story. Later he said he'd like an Englishman in it.' 'At first Ruth didn't want to bring a man into it so strongly, or at all,' Ivory said. 'And I said that I thought we could not have just a solitary woman. That wouldn't be interesting and why couldn't we have an Englishman who had some involvement with the court? It would give her another way of saying things. We agreed.' At the time she was writing *Autobiography of a Princess*, Ruth Jhabvala was also planning *Heat and Dust*, the novel which in 1975 won the Booker literary award. She tried out ideas in *Autobiography* which subsequently appeared in *Heat and Dust*.

**'Autobiography of a Princess':
James Mason, Madhur Jaffrey**

Ruth Jhabvala returned to Delhi, having discussed the script with Ivory in New York. 'I wrote the script from these elements: the footage of the palaces, the interviews, the old footage, the princess and an Englishman. The archive footage was eventually inserted as I indicated in the script. I saw some of this footage in Jodhpur and then Ismail showed me the whole lot in London together with the sequence they had shot with the old singer of Jaisalmer. I spent several days in the screening room looking at this terrible stuff. I just knew I had to have that wonderful sequence with the old woman and end with it.' At first, both Ivory and Ruth Jhabvala, who were away from London, had reservations about what appeared to them Merchant's precipitate casting of James Mason as the Englishman. Ivory had an image of James Mason as a glamorous sleek-haired movie star: an impression later confirmed in London by their first meeting over dinner at the Dorchester. 'All that night,' Ivory said, 'I tossed and turned, thinking I just couldn't go through with this. Night thoughts. We met at the flat which was our set for the day of rehearsal with the two actors. And from the moment Mason stepped out of his car he was in character: grey, nondescript, wearing an old man's sweater, creeping up the stairs, easing himself into a chair. Then he opened his mouth: we didn't have to make a single change. Letter perfect with wonderful pauses.'

Autobiography of a Princess observes the unities. Indeed, its 60-minute running time is not much more than that covered by the action of the plot. What is important is not the present but memory, the past recollected. A divorced Indian princess (played as intended by Madhur Jaffrey), resplendently jewelled, prepares for her annual tea party, a sumptuous Indian spread, with her late father's private secretary. He has travelled to London from a seaside town where he spends his retirement researching (but out of his Indian habits delaying writing) the life of an exemplary British official of the Raj, a collector of the history, poetry and song of the district he administered. The imperious princess, who has hired a projector to remind the Englishman, Cyril Sahib, of the long ago days at her father's court, would, however, have him write instead the life of her dashing, cruel, grandly preposterous and finally foolishly disgraced father. She wants the Englishman to pin down her heritage. Both the princess and Cyril Sahib are exiles. She is a Western-educated Indian, a 'modern girl', supposedly at home in London, but at heart still an Indian (she gives imperious orders to the boy who comes with the projector, automatically, without a second thought for his feelings), not understanding, getting beneath the skin of the English. Cyril Sahib is an Englishman who spent his working life in India, was seduced by ease and the kindness of the princess's father, but never really understood the country or understood it less the longer he stayed.

In the course of their teatime conversation, which is enlivened for us by her clips (a wedding, pig-sticking, a funeral), a suffocating lost world is conjured. As Ruth Jhabvala revealed in an unbroadcast interview for the BBC's *Lively Arts* programme, she strongly identified with Cyril Sahib, into whose mouth she put many of her feelings about India. She had lived there continuously, an outsider, for 23 years, and like him now felt herself on the point of being overwhelmed. 'He loved India at first,' she said, 'and then, as he got deeper and deeper into it, it frightened and then horrified him. He became more and more alienated, but after he returned to England he could again love India. This wasn't only my own experience. The Englishman was partly based on E. M. Forster and J. R. Ackerley who went out as secretaries to Maharajas in the 1920s but stayed only a short time. The last movement, the feeling of alienation, didn't happen to them.'

**'Autobiography of a Princess':
the singer of Jaisalmer**

p.c—MIP. *p*—IM. *d*—JI. *asst. d*—Nick Young. *sc*—RPJ. *continuity*—Christine Fox. *ph*—Walter Lassally. In colour. *ed*—Humphrey Dixon. *a.d*—Jacquemine Charrot-Lodwige; (asst.) Richard Macrory. *m*—Vic Flick. *sd. rec*—Bob Bentley. *cast*—James Mason (*Cyril Sahib*), Madhur Jaffrey (*the Princess*), Keith Varnier (*Delivery Man*), Diane Fletcher (*Seductress*), Timothy Bateson (*Blackmailer*), Johnny Stuart (*Photographer*), Nazrul Rahman (*Papa*). 59 mins. (16mm).

THE WILD PARTY

Raquel Welch, James Coco

Raquel Welch, James Coco, Perry King
Location: Riverside (California)
Shooting: May to June 1974
Premiere: None; Washington/Boston/Cincinnati, May 1974

The company's next feature, *The Wild Party*, which went into production at the Mission Inn at Riverside, in Southern California, soon after the shooting of *Autobiography*, did not have a happy passage. The story, adapted by Walter Marks and Ivory from a poem of 1928 by Joseph Moncure March, the journalist and one-time managing editor of the *New Yorker*, opens on the morning that silent film-maker Carlo Grimaldo (James Coco), known to the world as Jolly Grimm, is anxiously preparing a Hollywood party to premiere his make-or-break comeback, *Brother Jasper*, a sentimental comedy about the patron saint of California. His co-writer, the narrator of the film proper, is even more apprehensive: *Brother Jasper* contains scenes too broad ('You can't boil me, I'm a Friar,' Jolly quips to some cannibals) for the sophisticated audiences of the late 1920s. Jolly will hear no criticism: it's his picture; he has been in the business 20 years; he knows what his public wants. In the event, however, the picture does not win the hearts of the studio executives (one bearing a heavy resemblance to Louis B. Mayer) who as potential distributors have been cajoled and bribed into attendance. Jolly hits the bottle.

'The Wild Party': Ralph Manza, James Coco, Royal Dano

JI: No, there's more: It was bad enough that AIP had totally recut *The Wild Party* (only three scenes remained intact out of 60), and that Home Box Office preferred to buy that horribly messed-up, ugly and relentlessly sordid version of the film, which they broadcast. But later on NBC bought the original version, then proceeded to bowdlerise it, and in the process recut it as totally. Gutted it, you could say. Anything explicitly sexual came out and, of course, any nudity. Out came Jolly's swear words, even mild ones like 'Hell!' and 'For Christ's sake!' (too *irreverent*). Out came every reference to homosexuality. (But when the film was shown over NBC-affiliated stations in upstate New York – this was July 1976 – it was followed by an announcement of next week's film: *My Daughter Was a Teenage Lesbian*, or some such.) I don't know where the audience was going to find the 'wild' in that party, and they switched off in the millions, or never switched on. So, when people tell me that they saw the film on TV in the United States, I say, 'Oh, yes? I'm sorry.' However, sometimes they say they liked it anyway.

The Wild Party, which was produced under the banner of Samuel Z. Arkoff's American International Pictures, did not find favour with its distributor: AIP recut the film, against Ivory's wishes, added discarded footage with a view to enhancing the advertising catchline 'Hollywood in the 20s – a night they're still whispering about!' Ivory repudiated this version.* Some years later, however, Merchant Ivory Productions bought back distribution rights and the director's cut was re-released theatrically in Britain, and has since been rehabilitated in the United States as well. The full acrimonious story of the distribution fate of the AIP version of *The Wild Party* has been told by Ivory in *Index on Censorship* (Summer 1976). From the producer and the director's point of view, the actual production of the film was not helped by the uneasy relationship between themselves and their star, Raquel Welch, with whom Ivory said he was never able to develop a working relationship. They were unused to players who came with a large entourage and expected to be treated more 'respectfully' than other members of the cast and crew. There were 'scenes', reminiscent of Old Hollywood, and at one point the star temporarily quit the production. Ironically, however, little of this tension shows on screen.

The idea for *The Wild Party* had originated with the lyricist Walter Marks who had taken it to Edgar Lansbury and Joseph Beruh, the producers of *Godspell* and other Broadway musicals. Merchant Ivory entered the picture when Walter Marks' brother Peter, a New York art dealer, mentioned over lunch that his brother had an idea for a film but lacked a director. Lansbury and Beruh were shown *Savages* and liked it. Merchant and Ivory were duly hired. The notion of a 'musical' set in 20s Hollywood based on a narrative poem appealed to Ivory. However, Walter Marks' highly expressionistic and very lurid script required considerable work. James Coco had agreed to play Jolly subject to final approval of the script, and he was applying pressure for change. At the end of 1973, Ivory sent the script and a copy of the original poem to Ruth Jhabvala in Delhi who suggested, principally, how the triangular relationship between Jolly, his suffering mistress Queenie (Raquel Welch) and the coming star Dale Sword (Perry King) who woos her during the party, might be developed.

'Ruth was at that time busy with *Heat and Dust*,' Ivory said. 'As the script progressed, and it went through at least a couple of rewrites, I would send pieces of it to her. I had to be very careful. If an idea started with her, then I had to introduce it to Walter Marks as my idea. He never knew that there was this far-off lady sitting in India who was from time to time sending bits of scenario along which were going to get put into his script. Ruth didn't write any scenes but she did give very elaborate instructions for episodes that particularly interested her and then I wrote them. The scene in which Queenie explains what it was like when she first met Jolly was one of Ruth's: Queenie has been working in vaudeville and Jolly was the first person who took her seriously. All that was in Walter Marks' script but very underdeveloped. Ruth sowed seeds. There was one other scene which was in a way hers. An unlikely scene. At the party, Jolly is quite drunk and acts out a bank robbery. That was a collaboration between Walter Marks and Ruth with me in the middle.'

Ivory has recalled the familiarity of the settings for *The Wild Party*. 'I never really read movie magazines as a child, I just kind of imbibed them. For instance, I collected cards from packets of chewing gum. You licked the card, it had a rotten-egg taste, and then a movie star's face would come up. I loved those cards: Jean Harlow, Una Merkel, Warner Baxter. I can remember *Gold Diggers of 1933* and *42nd Street*. I can remember when *42nd Street* played in our town. I remember sitting on the front porch with my mother, and mother called out to a passing woman who replied "I can't stop now, I'm on my way to see *42nd Street*." We also had sheet music on the piano, and this was very often of Hollywood songs. On the cover would be the actor or actress, the typical Hollywood photograph of the day. All this left a residue which later on, I believe, became the stuff of *The Wild Party*. I looked at Jimmy Coco's collection of old fan magazines when it came time to make the movie and it all came back to me.'

Time has again moved on. A performer finds himself marooned – though unlike the Buckinghams, Jolly Grimm is able to mount a hard-fought rearguard action – in an age, the Talkies, which no longer have much use for him, for his style. The setting for his fall is a mansion redolent of old money, old in Hollywood terms, for Jolly is one of the Maharajas of this new worldwide civilisation. Like the real Maharajas, he still has one or two retainers, notably a chauffeur-cum-friend, a stuntman from the 'dusters', and a retinue which senses this is his last throw of the dice. Doug and Mary are giving another party that evening at Pickfair. Jolly's guests, the more important ones, are anxious to be off to it. They have come out of faintly embarrassed necessity, not wishing to show disrespect to the once famous comic in case his comeback picture proves a hit. They are, in a sense, trapped in Jolly's Chinese Hispanic mansion, as the house-guests are trapped in Carlotta's mansion. Both are witnesses to the old order crumbling. In *Shakespeare Wallah*, one was left with the feeling that the old order would in fact stumble along, that the Gleneagles Hotel would never have its glory restored, its wine-racks replenished, but that it would somehow survive. After Jolly's party, nothing, however, can be the same. The melodramatic killing at the end of *Bombay Talkie*, when Vikram's scriptwriter (and he has a similar distanced counterpart in *The Wild Party*) stabs the star to death, registers – as was intended – as an ironic reprise of one of the killings in a Vikram movie. In *The Wild Party*, Ivory was aiming not for melodrama but authentic tragedy.

Ivory's *Wild Party* was not a yellow sheet reconstruction of Roscoe Arbuckle's ill-fated wild party of 1921,* in the aftermath of which an actress died and

'The Wild Party': Annette Ferra, dancing

JI: What an idea! To make a musical out of the Arbuckle scandal. But that is what people think. We were actually offered Arbuckle's limousine for a scene in the film, but I couldn't do it.

71

'The Wild Party': James Coco and Raquel Welch (top balcony) make an entrance

Arbuckle was accused though not convicted of manslaughter. The surface similarities are evident: two fat comics gave a party and two women died – and Arbuckle was subsequently reduced to working under the pseudonym (almost as arch as 'Jolly Grimm') of Will B. Good. This wild party, however, is not really about identifiable people, even given the key off-screen presence of Fairbanks and Pickford, although it is about an almost too real Hollywood. The film is a cool meditation on Hollywood behaviour which has not changed greatly down the years: the shallowness of stardom, the venality (sexual and professional) of heartless executives, the fragility of fame, the rarity of loyalty and friendship. One scene in particular impresses itself. The audience is silenced and Jolly, in his newly tailored white jacket, steps before the curtains – in the way some film-makers do, to the embarrassment of preview or festival audiences – to say a few nervous words of explanation. The film rolls; laughter is uproarious and universal for the first gag, but then fitfully decreases; hidden, but not hidden at all, by the dark, the audience begins to shuffle, chatter, light cigarettes, make passes; Jolly knows in his heart that it's all over. The narrator, James Morrison, who watches Jolly during this painful episode with a look of sympathy, is an outsider, a literate college boy (read, if you choose, Scott Fitzgerald or James Ivory). His role is to observe and in the end, having been wounded in the shooting, when Jolly shoots Dale Sword and also succeeds in killing Queenie, to begin to turn his experiences not into *The Last Tycoon* but his own *Wild Party*.

p.c–Lansbury-Beruh/MIP. (A Samuel Z. Arkoff presentation. Released through American International Pictures.) *exec. p*–Edgar Lansbury, Joseph Beruh. *p*–IM. *d*–JI. *assoc. p*–George Manasse. *asst. d*–Edward Folger. *sc*–Walter Marks. Based on the narrative poem by Joseph Moncure March. *script supervisor*–Marilyn Giardino. *ph*–Walter Lassally. *col*–Movielab. *camera op*–Marcel Shayne. *ed*–Kent McKinney; (asst.) Courtney V. Hazell. *a.d*–David Nichols. *set dec*–Bruce David Weintraub. *set artist*–Pamela Gray. *sp. effects*–Edward Bash. *title poster art*–Peter Diaferia. *titles*–Arthur Eckstein. *stills*–Morgan Renard. *m/m.d*–Larry Rosenthal. *dance m*–Louis St Louis. *songs*–'The Wild Party', 'Funny Man', 'Not That Queenie of Mine', 'Singapore Sally', 'Herbert Hoover Drag', 'Ain't Nothing Bad About Feeling Good', 'Sunday Morning Blues' by Walter Marks. *choreo*–Patricia Birch. *cost*–(design) Ron Talsky; (James Coco, Perry King, David Dukes) Ralph Lauren; (Jennifer Lee, Dena Dietrich, Tiffany Bolling) Ronald Kolodgie; (wardrobe) Eric Kjemvik. *make-up*–Louis Lane. *hairstyles*–John Malone. *sd. ed*–Mary Brown. *sd. rec*–Gary Alper. *sd. re-rec*–Richard Vorisek. *stunt coordinator*–Teri McComas. *cast*–James Coco (*Jolly Grimm*), Raquel Welch (*Queenie*), Perry King (*Dale Sword*), Tiffany Bolling (*Kate*), Royal Dano (*Tex, Jolly's chauffeur*), David Dukes (*James Morrison*), Dena Dietrich (*Mrs Murchison*), Regis J. Cordic (*Mr Murchison*), Jennifer Lee (*Madeline True*), Marya Small (*Bertha*), Bobo Lewis (*Wilma*), Annette Ferra (*Nadine*), Eddie Laurence (*Kreutzer*), Tony Paxton (*Sergeant*), Waldo K. Berns (*Policeman*), Nina Faso (*Lady in Black*), Baruch Lumet (*Tailor*), Martin Kove (*Editor*), Ralph Manza (*Fruit Dealer*), Lark Geib (*Rosa*), Frederic Franklyn (*Sam*), J. S. Johnson (*Morris*), Michael Grant Hall (*Oscar D'Armano*), Skipper (*Phil D'Armano*), Don De Natale (*Jackie the Apache Dancer*), Tom Reese (*Eddy*), Geraldine Baron (*Grace*), Jill Giraldi (*Crippled Girl*), Barbara Quinn (*Mildred*), Gloria Gadhoke (*Redhead*), Clea Ariel, Susan Arnold, Joe Arrowsmith, Jonathan Becker, Waldo K. Berns, Bob Buckingham, Jennifer Chessman, Mark David Jacobson, Rick Kanter, Kevin Matthews, Luke Matthiessen, Gordon Maus, Bill Merickel, Tony Paxton, Anthony Pecoraro, Jack Sachs, Carmen Saveiros, Mark Swope, Ayesha Taft and Whitney Tower (*Party Guests*). 100 mins. (35mm).

SWEET SOUNDS

Location: Mannes College (New York City)
Shooting: July 1976
Premiere: New York Film Festival, October 1976

'Sweet Sounds'

In 1976, Merchant Ivory Productions backed a short film, *Sweet Sounds*, their second side project after *Helen, Queen of the Nautch Girls*. It was instigated by Richard Robbins who wished to make a record of some of the children and some of the teaching methods of New York's Mannes College of Music Preparatory School, of which he was then director. 'Dick Robbins,' Ivory said, 'who has since become a close collaborator, came into our lives via Firoza Jhabvala, Ruth's youngest daughter, a piano student in New York. Dick became her teacher and soon after, in 1976, met the rest of us. By the time we came to make *The Europeans*, in 1978, I trusted him enough to accept the idea of him composing the music for that film, though 'compose' is not perhaps quite accurate: he selected judiciously from various sources. By the time we had arrived at *Jane Austen in Manhattan*, in 1980, he was writing very original film music, notably the seven-minute opera *Sir Charles Grandison*, and he has since given me music as good as I've ever had.'*

Whereas *Helen* gave itself over to an exceptional popular entertainer, with 500 films behind her, *Sweet Sounds* gave itself over to a mixed class of ten pre-school children selected for their responsiveness to rhythm and pitch future professional musicians, perhaps – and to two ebullient teachers. The film, which cost some $25,000 and was edited by Humphrey Dixon, a regular MIP collaborator since the days of *The Guru*, was an engaging record of communicated enthusiasm. The children belie what appears occasionally to be a wandering lack of attention by the speed of their responses. A boy, eyes lowered, plays the cello with painful concentration; a small moment, highlighted by his application, which lodges in the mind. *Sweet Sounds*, an unaffected 'home movie', was screened at the New York and London festivals.

JI: Or let me put it another way: no one has given me any that I have liked *better*, except for the title music of *Shakespeare Wallah*, by Satyajit Ray. Like all good music directors (including Ray), Robbins has his own ideas and doesn't always do what I'd expect him to do. And since I am not a musician, he can't enlighten me beforehand, so I find out in the recording studio. This way of working with composers isn't very different from the way I work with actors, who also bring their particular vision to the project. This is as it should be, otherwise why hire them? You can't on the whole force your fellow artists to do anything on a film, and I don't try to. It's my job to create an atmosphere in which everybody is free to expand under my guidance. That may sound a bit like a hot house, but it's not a bad analogy.

p.c–MIP. *p*–IM. *d/sc*–Richard Robbins. *continuity*–Dorothea Swope. *ph*–Richard Inman Pearce, Fred Murphy. In colour. *ed*–Humphrey Dixon. *m*–Hai-Kung Suh (*piano*); Herbert Levine, Paul Twerdowsky (*guitar*), Nanette Levi (*violin*), Eugenie Dengel (*viola*), William Hanny (*cello*). *sd. rec*–Larry Loewinger. *p. crew*–Marc Rogers, Roger Dean, John Kelley. 29 mins. (16mm).

Don De Natale and partner

Chapter Four

DANCING PARTNERS

ROSELAND

Christopher Walken, Geraldine Chaplin, Lilia Skala, Teresa Wright
Location: New York City
Shooting: January to February and April 1977
Premiere: New York Film Festival, October 1977

While *Sweet Sounds* was in production, Ruth Jhabvala was writing a script based on her story 'How I Became a Holy Mother'. Merchant thought that the story, published in *Encounter* in February 1976, might make a suitable vehicle for the actress Irene Worth and hoped that the brothers Dennis and Michael Murphy, businessmen from Portland, Oregon, whose family had made a fortune in lumber, might be encouraged to invest in it. Ivory describes the Murphys as West Coast equivalents to the Kennedys, 'vigorous, rich, handsome, lordly'. 'I don't think they particularly wanted to go into film production, but there was no reason why they wouldn't either. First-time investors in films of course hope to make money, though few study the books that closely. But there is also the spur of excitement – people like to make movies, to be mixed up with stars.'

In the event, however, Michael Murphy was not fired by the *Holy Mother* script. A young American woman, the disciple of a benevolent guru (from the story one imagines him a close cousin to the sensuous cosseted guru of *Bombay Talkie*), is taken up by her master's dragonlike confederate, a titled lady with plans, transformed into a 'holy mother' (the consort of an enlightened younger guru) and transported about the world as a spiritual exhibit. The story was set in India, but the action was later transposed with the intention of filming in Oregon.* In search of a location for one brief New York scene, Ivory, Merchant and Ruth Jhabvala were taken by Don De Natale, who had played the Apache

JI: Our script, written in 1976 and set in a lakeside ashram in Oregon, wasn't nearly as fantastic or far-fetched as a latter-day, real-life migration. Bhagwan Shree Rajneesh, India's richest and most controversial swami, transported his ashram near Poona to Antelope in Eastern Oregon. The ashram bought land and its inmates now, in 1982, live somewhat uneasily in a tent city near there, warily – and somewhat resentfully – watched by the local inhabitants, mostly nononsense ranchers. It is reported that ashram members successfully ran for local office in an attempt to 'control' the region. There have been ugly confrontations and a show of guns; one is reminded somewhat of the Mormons' trek to the Great Salt Lake. 'How I Became a Holy Mother' was the mildest and gentlest of modern fables by comparison. Perhaps that was the reason that the project never got off the ground. Ruth sees gurus as, on the whole, benign presences, though with human weaknesses. Whereas I can't help seeing them as both sinister and comic.

JI: The idea for the magic mirror in the waltz story (in which the Teresa Wright character glimpses her younger self and her late partner) came from Nathaniel Hawthorne: 'Dr Heidegger's Experiment'. I had been reading Hawthorne's short stories to get myself ready for a television adaptation of 'My Kinsman, Major Molineux', which I was to direct in 1976 but which was then not made. 'Dr Heidegger's Experiment' interested me and I showed it to Ruth who liked it too. This is a story about two old men and an old woman whom they both loved when they were young. All drink Dr Heidegger's magic elixir and, becoming young again, their appetites for brawling and sex soon get the better of them. But then the effects of the elixir begin to wear off and the trio shrivel up à la *Lost Horizon*. In Hawthorne's story, these transformations are reflected in a mirror. So magic mirrors were very much in our minds that year. It was probably naive of us to think we could employ that kind of storytelling device in a film made today. But if there *were* such things as magic mirrors, they would certainly be found in the Roseland ballroom.

dancer in *The Wild Party*, to Roseland, the famous old New York ballroom. Could it not, they wondered, also be used as the location for a film? Its elderly habituees had stories to tell, had reasons for being there. *How I Became a Holy Mother* was abandoned – only the second of Ruth Jhabvala's completed scripts for MIP not to have been realised – and Michael Murphy, following in the steps of Joseph Saleh, was persuaded to back a Roseland film on the strength of an enthusiastic sketch of the plot. Before this, however, Merchant had to persuade Ivory and Ruth Jhabvala, who were dragging their feet. Was Roseland, they wondered, where they really wanted to be?

In March 1976, Ruth Jhabvala set up a second home in Manhattan, taking an apartment in the East 50s, in the same building in which Merchant and Ivory had their home base. Her summers were henceforth usually spent in New York. 'For some time,' she said, 'India had been becoming too much for me. In 1975, with my daughters grown up, it became feasible for me to leave for part of the year.' (In her Neil Gunn lecture, Ruth Jhabvala has described her desperate homesickness for Europe – the European state of mind – after twenty-four years in India.) She was, however, already a refugee from Europe, and like many of her fellow refugees from that continent she considered New York the place for which she was destined. 'Certainly, when I first went there, in 1966, I felt a sense of homecoming. It is the most European city I can think of...' In September, after further visits to the ballroom, she began the script of *Roseland*. It was composed in the form of three short stories, an intricate central episode, 'The Hustle', flanked by two more straightforward two-handers, 'The Waltz' and 'The Peabody', both concerned with elderly women, sentimentalists but not finally self-pitying, each of whom has lost her dancing partner. 'The Hustle', buttressed by these intimations of mortality, concerns a handsome young man who is variously claimed by three very different women. They want him as a cushion against the uncertainties of the future rather than as a touchstone to the past. 'Did I act as a fly on the wall?' Ruth Jhabvala asked. 'Yes, I just sat there. I am not at all good at speaking to people. They had to be brought up to me and told: "Tell her! Tell her something interesting." I'm not good at eliciting responses. I stared at them and they stared back. Oh! I wouldn't make much of an interviewer, but I like to listen.'*

'When Ruth first came to live in New York,' Ivory said, 'she had already written American stories, mainly about New Yorkers, but I don't think she felt ready to write a novel set in America, even though she had been coming to the United States off and on since 1966. Roseland, however, was different. It was much simpler. People ran to type; they had similar stories; they were there for similar reasons. It wasn't, I think, all that difficult for her to pick up. Ruth has said that Roseland wasn't her "scene", or mine. But in a way it *was* my scene, even though I had walked past it hundreds of times and never dreamed of going in. I was very snooty. Once inside, however, Roseland did powerfully

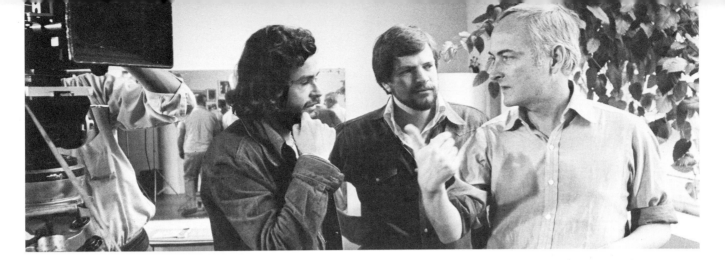

'Roseland': cameraman Ernest
Vincze (left) and James Ivory
in the ballroom.

remind me of my youth. When I was a junior and senior in high school, three evenings a week, every week, we would go to the armory in Klamath Falls and dance to Baldy's Band. It was the end of the war and there were servicemen and older women. It was the same kind of dancing that they did at Roseland, the same atmosphere, the same soft lights, the same music. I'd seen all that 25 years before: the same people, in a sense, except that they had all gone grey. In Oregon, as at Roseland, it was all very respectable. Nobody came in drunk. Parents knew their children would be safe.'

Ruth Jhabvala was relieved to have the opportunity to create characters who spoke English, and who spoke to other people who spoke English. 'Writing dialogue for Indians wasn't difficult, but it did call for an artificial convention, since most of the time they wouldn't have been speaking English.' And this relief found expression in the complexity of the film's central episode, the most sustained, psychologically shaded and 'written' passage that had to date found its way into a Merchant Ivory film. Speaking about the 'double pretence' from within which *Heat and Dust*, her final novel composed in India, had been written, Ruth Jhabvala isolated a central difficulty: 'On the one hand, as far as the Indian characters and their society and thoughts and values were concerned, I pretended to be of them; on the other hand, when I wrote about the Anglo-Indian (that is, British) characters and their traditions, I pretended to be of *them*.' In reality, she was part of neither tradition; in *Roseland*, she found she was addressing people rooted in (or uprooted from) the same soil as herself.

In *Autobiography of a Princess*, she had described – rather than dramatised – that singular state of mind, of disinheritance, which marooned an educated Indian woman in England 'at home' in London but not really understanding the English, not understanding what they meant behind what they said. In *Roseland*, despite the fact that they are emigrants or the children of emigrants, have come from different countries, the characters understand each other, and in some cases only too well. They suffer sometimes from a debilitating excess of

'Roseland': Floyd Chisholm,
Annette Rivera

'Roseland': Christopher Walken, Joan Copeland

empathy for one another. When, in 'The Peabody', a formidable German lady (Lilia Skala) expresses exasperation with the efforts of her mouselike partner – she wants more than anything to win the Champagne Hour, the Peabody competition, to regain the past; he has a doubtful heart, can't find the steps – the exasperation strikes home unequivocally. At Roseland, where mannerly behaviour is required, people sometimes conceal their feelings out of deference, but they are not on the whole closed books.

Roseland was photographed by Ernest Vincze, whose second feature it was. What distinguishes the film is both the conjuring of the ballroom, a rather sombre, cavernous place (everything seemed designed for more people) but one still, like the Maharajas' palaces, capable of putting on a show, and the sense of contemporary individuals speaking out and speaking from the heart. The rich woman of a certain age (Joan Copeland) who is anxious to hang on to her particular taxi-dancer (Christopher Walken), half gigolo and half – she wants to believe – friend for friendship's sake; her younger friend (Geraldine Chaplin) who cannot understand why the young man will not throw in with her ('You cannot,' he says, 'have everything you want') and the young man's former dance-teacher and lover (Hellen Gallagher) – the Ivory/Jhabvala outsider – who wants to turn back the clock but knows in truth she can't. They all have a present history, get by with a certain muscularity, submit to compromise. Ruth Jhabvala has spoken of the 'tough, fighting, thinking European or, more often, American girls' – often described in her writing – who went to India to seek enlightenment only to give up their personalities. The people of Roseland have their personalities intact. Unlike MIP's preceding American film, *Roseland* is not distanced by a period setting. Returning to their past, in India, as MIP were to do in their next feature, was to prove difficult after such a radical break.

---

p.c–MIP. In association with the Oregon Four. *p*–IM. *d*–JI. *exec. p*–Michael T. Murphy, Ottomar Rudolf. *assoc. p*–Dennis J. Murphy, Macy Wall. *p. co-ordinator*–Lisa Harris. *p. manager*–Jeff Bricmont. *asst. d*–David Appleton, Ted Devlin. *sc/story*–RPJ. *ph*–Ernest Vincze. *col*–Movielab. *ed*–Humphrey Dixon, Richard Schmiechen. *a.d*–(uncredited). *m/m. arranger/m.d*–Michael Gibson. *songs*–'Rocking Chair' by Hoagy Carmichael; 'Baubles, Bangles and Beads', 'Stranger in Paradise' by Robert Wright, George Forrest; 'The Moon and Manakoora' by Franklin Loesser, Alfred Newman; 'On a Slow Boat to China' by Frank Loesser; 'Super Cool' by Elton John, Bernie Taupin, performed by Cheryl Lynn. *cost*–Dianne Finn Chapman. *dance d*–Patricia Birch. *titles*–R. Greenberg Associates. *sd. rec*–Cabell Smith. *sd. re-rec*–Jack Higgins. *sd.*

effects–Jill Demby. *p. assistants*–Mark Potter Jr, Janet E. Fishman, Debbie Cohen, Chris Adler, Julia Keydel, Richard Numeroff, Wiley Wood, Mark David Jacobson. *l.p*–'The Waltz': Teresa Wright (*May*), Lou Jacobi (*Stan*), Don De Natale (*Master of Ceremonies*), Louise Kirkland (*Ruby*), Hetty Galen (*Red Haired Lady*), Carol Culver (*Young May*), Denny Shearer (*Eddie*); 'The Hustle': Geraldine Chaplin (*Marilyn*), Hellen Gallagher (*Cleo*), Joan Copeland (*Pauline*), Christopher Walken (*Russel*), Conrad Janis (*George*), Jayne Heller (*Bella*), Annette Rivera and Floyd Chisholm (*Hustle Couple*), Jeanmarie Evans (*Cloakroom Attendant*); 'The Peabody': Lilia Skala (*Rosa*), David Thomas (*Arthur*), Edward Kogan (*Bartender*), Madeline Lee (*Camille*), Stan Rubin (*Bert*), Dortha Duckworth (*Ladies' Room Attendant*). 104 mins. (35mm).

HULLABALOO OVER
GEORGIE AND BONNIE'S PICTURES

At the door of the treasure house

Aparna Sen, Victor Banerjee, Peggy Ashcroft, Saeed Jaffrey, Larry Pine
Location: Jodhpur
Shooting: February 1978
Premiere: London Weekend Television, September 1978

'The story,' Ruth Jhabvala said in a 'discussion' between herself, Ismail Merchant and James Ivory (written by them and published in the *New York Times*, 5 October 1980), 'is about a collection of Indian miniature paintings kept hidden away in a Maharaja's palace. The characters are, on the one hand, the easy-going Maharaja who wants to keep his pictures, and his beautiful greedy sister who wants to sell them; and on the other, the various people striving to get possession of these pictures – the formidable English lady [Peggy Ashcroft] with a mingled stream of Memsahib, adventuress and art-lover's blood flowing in her veins; the American connoisseur, shrewd, daring and predatory as a robber baron [part, by his admission, the film director and picture collector James Ivory]; the Indian dealer of the merchant caste for whom buying and selling – the object may be soap or precious paintings – is his traditional life-fulfilment.'

Melvyn Bragg, the novelist, interviewed Ruth Jhabvala for the BBC in the

'Hullabaloo Over Georgie and Bonnie's Pictures': Victor Banerjee

summer of 1977. He was about to move to the *South Bank Show*, the London Weekend Television arts programme which he had recently joined as presenter. Would Ivory, he asked after the interview, consider making a film for the programme, subject open, but with some 'arts' connection? Ivory would; the subject of collecting Indian miniature paintings was eventually settled on after other subjects were developed, then dropped for being either impractical or tedious to make. Ivory had twenty years' experience collecting Indian pictures in India and elsewhere and knew the dealer-collector-museum axis.* LWT agreed to put up a major part of the production cost. Not having made a picture in India for eight years, however, MIP underestimated the cost of the venture which came out at £250,000. During the autumn, Ivory and Ruth Jhabvala tussled with a script: it seemed to them impossibly intractable and at one point, in Ivory's absence, Ruth Jhabvala vainly begged Merchant to release them from the task. The script was never properly finished.

Ivory: 'Even as the plane with Peggy Ashcroft, Walter Lassally and everybody else hired to make the film was approaching India's shores, Ruth was wringing her hands and saying she wanted to abandon it. We sat in her garden in Delhi trying to decide what to *do*. With the story, that is. We were still trying to figure out the denouement on location at the Umaid Bhavan palace in Jodhpur. Ruth would send anxious letters about the script or she'd telephone and we'd be cut off . . . It was a bit like *Savages*: we just kept shooting from these random bits of paper and hoped for the best.' After the film was finished, Merchant prevailed upon a reluctant Ruth Jhabvala to accompany him to the first London screening. 'We went with friends, who liked it,' she said. 'I have never been so utterly astonished. I couldn't see it at all.' Ironically, considering the extent of the critical praise the film subsequently received in Britain after it was shown on television, both Ivory and Ruth Jhabvala tend slightly to deprecate it: it is not among their favourites.

The film-makers gave a somewhat more politic account of the conception of *Hullabaloo Over Georgie and Bonnie's Pictures* in their *New York Times* discussion. At first two stories were envisioned and sketched out for LWT. One, set in the 19th century, was to be about 'those brave and somewhat pushy Englishwomen' who travelled through the Indian princely states doing watercolours and keeping journals; the other, a hundred years later, was to be about the planning (more feasible for MIP than the building) of an 'Art Deco folly in the sands of Rajasthan'. 'There was to be a lot of cross-cultural confusion and romance,' Ivory said. 'At the end, World War Two would start and the protagonists would all be scattered like the architect's mad plans – the kind of entertaining, pleasant story set in the British Raj that Hollywood used to do so well, the difference being that the production would never have ventured beyond California, and the studio *would* have built the most splendid set.' (The past had been kept alive in *Shakespeare Wallah*; lived through in *Savages*; recollected in

JI: No doubt film directors do like to think of themselves as shrewd, daring and predatory. In some respects I *was* the model for Clark Haven, but I was always more of an antlike collector, diligently and ceaselessly bearing away to safety various fallen tasty morsels. The real model was someone else (inasmuch as there are ever models in good fiction): Stuart Cary Welch Jr, the Boston art collector and connoisseur-scholar. When Clark Haven unwraps Georgie's pictures and starts to enthuse, it was Welch who supplied the running commentary – enraptured and witty – that Haven speaks. We knew we could never improve on Welch's sentences: they are the product of a lifetime of looking at works of art, and here he – Welch – was meditating on his own miniatures, which we photographed for the film. In another connection, Welch's writing on Indian pictures, which is the expression of his feeling for India (*A Flower from Every Meadow*) was one of the many influences – like music in the air, or a scent you might say – on Ruth when she was preparing to write *Heat and Dust*.

80

Autobiography of a Princess; assumed – by Jolly Grimm – still to exist in *The Wild Party*; and fantasised in *Roseland*. But the juxtaposition of past and present was not in fact to occur in *Hullabaloo*, and their fully realised interweaving would have to wait until MIP's 1982 film *Heat and Dust*.)

Elements of these two stories were retained in the final script, notably in the figure of Lady Gee, the widow of the Viceroy's ADC, who was, she related, undaunted by Pathan bandits and proved herself quite as unscrupulous in pursuit of the priceless Tasveer collection as her WASPishly cultured young rival Clark Haven (Larry Pine). The art of intriguing threads through several MIP films, and it is one of the things which the company invariably brings off with a light touch. *Hullabaloo Over Georgie and Bonnie's Pictures* is MIP's most accomplished exercise in the art and perils of intrigue. The tone of the film is perfectly caught in its title: the owners of the pictures, the Maharaja and his sister the Maharani (Victor Banerjee and Aparna Sen), still answer to the childhood nicknames bestowed upon them by their Scottish nanny.* The celebration of incongruities is another MIP forte which finds expression in the film. Georgie fools his guests, Haven and Lady Gee (his real guests as opposed to the paying guests, the tourists, who occupy one wing of his palace – and one can play English country-house tricks on real guests), by second guessing their scheme to feed drugged sweetmeats to the guard of the picture collection. The scene is amusing in itself, but the effect is heightened by having the guard a mute giant and Georgie dressed as Santa Claus.

What makes this film something much more than a merely captivating light comedy is its tone and subtext. In *The Guru*, India was for all the beauty of the Ganges a sinister and destructive country; in *Hullabaloo*, it is still destructive – the heat, dust and ants are inexorably destroying the miniature paintings – but the destructiveness is seen as somehow acceptable. To take a small example, the plumbing in the palace may be uncertain, bathroom fixtures may come away in the hand, but the great thing (and most of the Western characters seem to acknowledge this) is not to let oneself become preoccupied by these frustrations. The vagaries of the Indian character to outsiders – and Ruth Jhabvala, who now found herself to an extent an outsider, a part-New Yorker, was capable of writing about India with less rancour than in *Autobiography of a Princess* – are still infuriating vagaries; they are recorded, however, with tolerant affection.

The film is also infused with a fondness for the past, the 'Indian' India of the Raj, not previously evident in MIP's Indian films. The palace is haunted by the ghost of an English girl, a palace guest who had mysteriously disappeared after a dance in the 1920s and whose body had been found next morning in the purdah car (one of those grand vintage motorcars which appear in several MIP films); but, Lady Gee says, she likes to think that the girl died from 'an excess of happiness'. Unlike the melancholy Buckinghams, Lady Gee looks back on the

'Hullabaloo Over Georgie and Bonnie's Pictures': the Maharaja and the choir

JI: The whole time we were shooting *Hullabaloo* in Jodhpur, Aparna Sen was planning to direct her own film, *36 Chowringhee Lane*. She used to tell us about it, and we'd say, making dinner conversation, 'Oh, that sounds nice, Aparna, etc.' We'd see her lying on a marble bench in the garden, heels kicking in the soft night air, lost in some sort of reverie, and think, 'What a funny girl!'

'Hullabaloo Over Georgie and Bonnie's Pictures': Larry Pine (top), Peggy Ashcroft

past not so much nostalgically – she has after all a great deal of adventuring to do in the present – but with a genuine open-eyed affection: like the girl who died, she remembers the great days of Georgie and Bonnie's palace with an excess of happiness. Memory keeps the girl alive. And it is memory, finally, which will preserve the pictures. They are twice breathtakingly unwrapped for our pleasure; they are, however, chiefly an idea, a conception of beauty and perfection. The palace is the home of the idea and to remove them from it, from the culture however adulterated which gave birth to the idea, is at once to preserve the pictures and destroy them.

Hullabaloo is not a treatise on Art versus Life, the meaning of Art, the history of Indian miniature painting – which is not to say that the film does not have thoughts on these subjects. After Shri Narain (Saeed Jaffrey), the keeper of the Maharaja's pictures, has shown Lady Gee his 'private' collection of miniatures and she has pooh-poohed his reluctance to show her his erotica, a veiled woman enters and prepares a delicacy. Lady Gee lifts the veil, as she had lifted the tissue paper covering the miniatures, and reveals a plump smiling face. 'This,' Shri Narain declares, 'is my most precious and private collection.'

'When we "set fire" to a room in the Umaid Bhavan Palace,' Ivory said, 'for the climactic scene in which the miniatures apparently burn up, and damaged a stone window frame, life seemed to imitate art when the real Maharani waved away our expressions of dismay and sorrow with a supreme gesture of aristocratic nonchalance and as one who has a thousand other windows, saying it didn't matter, that a little plaster-of-Paris would fix up everything. But it did matter, for we left that palace, finished only in 1946, worse than we found it. It had been in pristine condition, and a film crew headed by an American director as intent on making his film and the cost be damned as the American collector of the story was intent on rifling his host's storeroom, became the first barbaric invasion to descend on one of India's greatest palaces. It was only a chip lost, but we knocked that chip out as surely as if we had fired a cannon at the ramparts.' Ismail Merchant: 'Oh that's all nonsense. We didn't leave the palace worse than we found it. We made our film there and just enhanced it.'

p.c–MIP. For London Weekend Television. *p*–IM. *d*–JI. *exec. p*–Melvyn Bragg. *p. assoc*–Nick Young, Vijay Amarani. *asst. d*–Javed Siddique. *sc*–RPJ. *ph*–Walter Lassally. *col*–Eastman Color. *ed*–Humphrey Dixon. *sets*– Bansi Chandragupta. *m*–Vic Flick. *poem*–'Waillie, Waillie' (anon) recited by Jenny Beavan. *cost*–Jenny Beavan, Purnima Agarwal. *make-up*–Mohamed Amir. *sd. rec*–Bob Bentley. *sd. re-rec*–Tony Anscombe. *l.p*–Peggy Ashcroft (*Lady Gwyneth McLaren Pugh, known as Lady Gee*), Larry Pine (*Clark Haven*), Saeed Jaffrey (*Shri Narain*), Victor Banerjee (*The Maharaja of Tasveer, known as 'Georgie'*), Aparna Sen (*The Maharani of Timarpur, known as 'Bonnie'*), Jane Booker (*Lynn/Joyful Girl*), Shamsuddin (*Deaf-mute*), Jenny Beavan (*Governess*), Aladdin Langa (*Servant*), the choir of The Sacred Heart of St Mary's, Jodhpur. 83 mins. (16mm).

THE EUROPEANS

New England registers the arrival of Europe

Lee Remick, Robin Ellis, Tim Woodward, Wesley Addy, Lisa Eichhorn
Locations: New Ipswich (N.H.), Salem (MA)
Shooting: October to November 1978
Premiere: Cannes Film Festival, May 1979

The success of *Hullabaloo Over Georgie and Bonnie's Pictures* in Britain encouraged the National Film Finance Corporation in 1978 to underwrite an adaptation of the novel *The Europeans* – subtitled by its author, Henry James, 'A Sketch' – which Ruth Jhabvala, a faithful Jamesian, had written several years before. Ivory recalls that in 1966 when Ruth Jhabvala learned that he had never seriously read Henry James, she remarked, 'But Jim, he could have been writing for *you.*' Ivory subsequently became an admirer – *The Spoils of Poynton* remains a favourite – but it was, he said, Ruth Jhabvala who was the consistent advocate of a film of *The Europeans*. Backers, however, had not at first materialised, despite the modest scale of the undertaking: there was no need for the elaborate reconstruction of long-vanished cities; the film could be done in two country houses in the New England countryside, with the merest glimpse of Boston's intact 19th-century streets and squares; there would be a small cast and few extras. James' biographer Leon Edel liked the script but that year's review panel of the National Endowment for the Arts in Washington, to

'The Europeans': Lee Remick, Wesley Addy

83

JI: James described Eugenia thus: 'She was not pretty … neither was she in her first youth; yet, though slender, with a great deal of extremely well-fashioned roundness of contour – a suggestion both of maturity and flexibility – she carried her three-and-thirty years as a light-wristed Hebe might have carried a brimming wine cup. Her complexion was fatigued, as the French say; her mouth was large, her lips too full, her teeth uneven, her chin rather commonly modelled; she had a thick nose … her forehead was very low … and she had a great abundance of crisp dark hair, finely frizzled, which was always braided in a manner that suggested some Southern or Eastern, some remotely foreign woman. She had a large collection of earrings, and wore them in alternation; and they seemed to give a point to her Oriental or exotic aspect…' In other words, plump, plain and – for 1850 – a woman of a 'certain age'. But James said too that she had beautiful, brilliant, intelligent eyes. She charmed with these, and with her manner, which was sophisticated and Continental. In the 1930s and early 40s this would have been a Bette Davis part – the only one in all my films – and she would have enjoyed playing that kind of clever *jolie laide*. She made the same impression on me when I was growing up that Eugenia made on the Wentworth clan. Like the Baroness Münster, she could mystify and terrify and I admired her sophistication, the stylish way she moved and dressed and lit her cigarette, the tart delivery of her acid lines, all of which I suppose seemed a long way from any woman I would ever have known in Klamath Falls. My knees would have turned to jelly of course if I had ever met someone like that.

whom MIP applied for partial funding in the hope of presenting the film on Public Television, was less enthusiastic: the novel, in the view of one scholar on the panel, was not a good one. Nevertheless, with the NFFC now behind it, the project found American and European backers, including Polytel, the West German production company. A few days before filming was to start, however, the principal American backer withdrew and there was a desperate, finally successful, scramble to find a replacement. Money held up through the shooting and editing; the only small hiccup before the film's profitable release in Britain was the contention over its registration as a British entry in the 1979 Cannes Film Festival.

The Europeans, which was shot in New England with a mainly British crew and a mainly American cast for a cost of £450,000, was like *Hullabaloo* a miniaturist piece about collectors. The film, which adheres to the tone and substance of the novel, opens with the arrival of the spirited Felix Young, a painter who has recently sailed from Europe with his sister Eugenia, the Baroness Münster, at the rural house of their respectable New England cousins, the Wentworths. Felix and Eugenia are soon installed as their cousins' guests. When Eugenia (Lee Remick), separated from her German husband and on the lookout for another, seems about to faint away at the mere thought of being at last among her kinfolk, Mr Wentworth (Wesley Addy), who is not for a moment duped, can do no less than offer the Europeans shelter in a house next door to his own. But they have designs on their hosts which require some intriguing. Eugenia is subtle, Felix forthright. The trouble is that, like Georgie, Mr Acton (Robin Ellis), on whom Eugenia has half set her heart, is no hayseed. She overplays her hand and loses him. Her brother, on the other hand, succeeds in obtaining permission to marry Mr Wentworth's troublesome daughter Gertrude; Mr Brand, the Unitarian minister who had hoped to marry her, is safely paired off with Gertrude's pious sister Charlotte; and the sisters' ne'er-do-well brother Clifford – the third of Mr Wentworth's miniature paintings – is in the end set safely on the road to a sober life in company with Mr Acton's sister Lizzie. As for Eugenia and Mr Acton, they are both left with an unresolved feeling of relief and regret.

'There is hardly a character in the film who is the ideal of the book,' Ivory said, 'with the possible exception of Mr Wentworth and maybe Charlotte.* When people say the film is so literary, I don't see how you can make a Henry James film, faithfully, and not be literary. It can't not be, for better or worse. However, the film for me has always been a very visual one, and not just because of all the autumn leaves. I just feel it is something you see rather than something you hear. What you see is the main thing; what you hear is the ornamentation. Some people may think that's crazy and it should be the other way round. But I was recently listening to all those lines and, wonderful though they are, there is nothing naturalistic about them and there is no naturalistic way of speaking them. It seemed that everybody thought before they said anything; then once something was said, it had to be thought about before a reply could be given.'

'The particular danger with this script,' Ruth Jhabvala said, 'was all the marvellous Henry James dialogue. I cut it down and then, after I reread it, I found I'd still kept in too much. I changed the way the story develops. You have to build to something central, something big. The novel is a succession of small scenes which don't build up to anything in particular. We added a ball at Mr Acton's house to which everything builds up, and from which everything then comes down. Everything from various parts of the novel is pulled together here. Henry James obviously rings bells with me. The feeling I had about Europeans coming to India, he had about Americans going to Europe. Everything he wrote has always struck particular bells.'

One of the pleasures of *The Europeans* – which was the first of MIP's films to find a substantial theatrical audience in both Europe and the United States – is its glancing observations: the pain on Mr Wentworth's carefully composed features when he contemplates his guests; the sweating earnestness of Mr Brand; the discomfiture of Eugenia, used, one imagines, to the grandeur of European balls, when faced with the prospect, at Mr Acton's party, of having to converse with a roomful of elderly aunts; the flurries of nervous excitement which overtake Charlotte when she is asked to intercede with her father on Gertrude's behalf. Ivory conveys too, particularly through the vivacious Lizzie Acton, the sense of the New World being a match for the scheming ways of the Old. What the films lacks – could perhaps never have – is the Jamesian voice; the novel is authentically unadaptable – and James himself found that he could not write effective dialogue for the stage. For all its engaging sidelong playfulness, the beauty of its settings, some excellent performances, there is in Ivory's *Europeans* also a sense of genuine characters trapped somewhat awkwardly by the conventions of their lines.*

'The Europeans': Lisa Eichhorn (left), Nancy New

JI: If you think about it for a moment, you can't help remembering that the lines of almost all period films – not counting Shakespeare and the classic playwrights like him – have conformed to the conventions of present-day speech. We accept this: ancient Greeks or Frenchmen speaking modern, even colloquial English, and so on. It's not realistic, but we accept it. We tried, however, to change all that in *The Europeans*, and made our characters conform to the conventions of American speech of the mid-19th century, as James wrote it. The public had no trouble with this feature of the film and apparently enjoyed it: the 'quaintness' of the language was like the 'quaintness' of everything else. It seemed a virtue, like the poke-bonnets. But for all that, James' delightful dialogue was *written*, intended to be savoured on the page, as opposed to *spoken*. They aren't the same, and the most gifted actors can't make them sound the same. This is probably where the trouble lies for some who saw the film.

p.c–MIP. With the National Film Finance Corporation. *p*–IM. *d*–JI. *assoc. p*–Connie Kaiserman. *p. manager*–Joyce Herlihy. *location manager*–Peter Kean. *asst. d*–Jim Maniolas, Christine Fox. *sc*–RPJ. Based on the novel by Henry James. *ph*–Larry Pizer. In colour. *ed*–Humphrey Dixon. *a.d*–Jeremiah Rusconi. *m*–Richard Robbins; 'Trio', Op. 17, by Clara Schumann, 'Deutsche Tanz', Op. 33, No. 7, by Franz Schubert, 'Schomberg Gallop' by G. W. E. Friedrich, 'Waltz' from *La Traviata* by Giuseppe Verdi, 'Old Folk Quadrilles', 'French Quadrilles' by Stephen Foster, 'Simple Gifts' traditional Shaker Hymn, 'Beautiful River' by Robert Lowry. *m.d/m. arranger*–Vic Flick. *choreo*–Elizabeth Aldrich, Charles Garth. *cost*–Judy Moorcroft. *make-up*–Jeanne Richmond, Marianne Grigg. *title art*–Mark Potter Snr, Trevor Bond. *titles*–Hillsberg & Meyer *sd*–Derek Ball. *sd. ed*–Brian Blamey. *sd. re-rec*–Doug Turner, Bob Jones. *p. assistants*–Michael Fields; Walter Bursiel, Ellen Dinerstein, Anthony Chase, Karen Shashoua, Steve Bach, John Rusconi. *l.p*–Lee Remick (*Eugenia, Baroness Münster*), Robin Ellis (*Robert Acton*), Tim Woodward (*Felix*), Wesley Addy (*Mr Wentworth*), Lisa Eichhorn (*Gertrude Wentworth*), Nancy New (*Charlotte Wentworth*), Tim Choate (*Clifford Wentworth*), Kristin Griffith (*Lizzie Acton*), Helen Stenborg (*Mrs Acton*), Norman Snow (*Mr Brand*), Gedda Petry (*Augustine*), James Ivory (*Man in Warehouse*). 83 mins. (35mm).

'Quartet': Maggie Smith

'Hullabaloo': Saeed Jaffrey, Peggy Ashcroft

'The Europeans': Tim Woodward

THE FIVE FORTY-EIGHT

Mary Beth Hurt, Laurence Luckinbill
Locations: New York City, Massachusetts, New Jersey
Shooting: August 1979
Premiere: Channel 13, New York City, November 1979

'The Five Forty-Eight': Mary Beth Hurt, Laurence Luckinbill

JI: It was intriguing for me to make *The Five Forty-Eight* back-to-back with *The Europeans*. I couldn't help feeling as we shot Cheever's story that its characters – unhappy, surfeited by a rich American lifestyle, at loose ends in their emotional lives, demoralised (literally lacking Mr Wentworth's 'moral grounds')–were the direct descendants of James' austere and principled New Englanders. Matters had proceeded with terrible inevitability in the 130 years since the earlier story took place, to land the Blakes and people like them in the misery with which Cheever presents them in his Shady Hill stories.

The Europeans was finished in spring 1979, shortly after which Ivory was approached by Channel 13 in New York to direct – independently of Merchant Ivory Productions – an adaptation by the playwright Terence McNally of the John Cheever story 'The 5:48'. It was to be one of a series of three; but because it involved a substantial amount of filming on board a train, it was the only one to be shot on film. The interest of this thriller – Blake, a loathsome advertising man (Laurence Luckinbill), is held up at gunpoint on the 5:48 train home from Grand Central Station to Shady Hill in Westchester County by his former secretary (Mary Beth Hurt), whom he has been to bed with and abandoned – is its proof that Ivory could handle with effect a writer very different in his manner of address from Ruth Jhabvala. People, for Ruth Jhabvala, have their reasons. The bold, accurately caricatured streak of hypocritical cruelty which runs through the ad man's character – and which is relished by both Cheever and Ivory – is entirely foreign to her characters.

The Five Forty-Eight is a slight film in the sense that the conclusion, with the girl humiliating the man rather than shooting him in cold blood, comes as little surprise. Manners; the mask put on and so casually taken off by the ad man; small moments of gratuitous cruelty; the perfectly timed insincere compliment; the tactics of unfriendliness towards one's neighbour, are what make up the fabric of the film – and which are the stuff of television drama. The girl's implied mental instability – she has just come out of hospital when she is taken on, desperate for a job, by the ad man – is only lightly sketched; the reasons for the ad man's heartlessness to his wife, his children and the women with whom he philanders are similarly treated. This is a moral tale: the characters, for all the surface detail of their lives, are chiefly ciphers.*

p.c–Channel 13. *p*–Peter Weinberg. *d*–JI. *exec. p*–Jac Venza. *assoc. p*–Steve Fairchild. *p. manager*–Joan Clancy. *location co-ordinator*–Susie Simons. *asst. d*–David Appleton. *sc*–Terrence McNally. Based on the story by John Cheever. *ph*–Andrzej Bartkowiak. In colour. *a.d*–John Wright Stevens. *cost*–Julie Weiss. *make-up*–Arlette Greenfield. *hair*–Joe Tubens. *cast*–Laurence Luckinbill (*John Blake*), Mary Beth Hurt (*Jane Dent*), Laurinda Barrett (*Louise Blake*), John DeVries (*Henry Watkins*), Robert Hitt (*Price*), Ann McDonough (*June Thorpe*), Philip Scher (*Charlie Blake*), Kathy Keeney (*Virginia Blake*), Nicholas Luckinbill (*Tad Watkins*), John Harkins (*Trace Beardon*). 58 mins. (16mm).

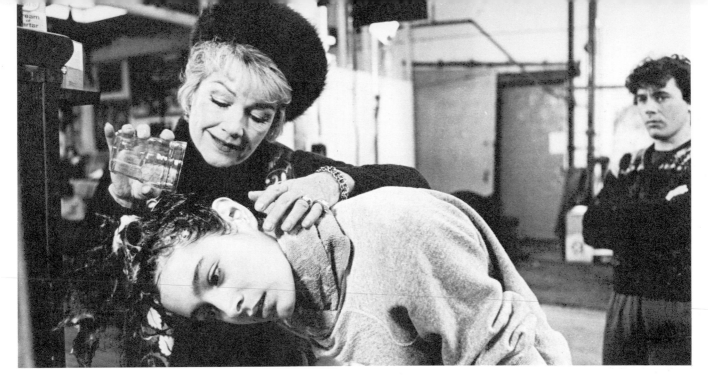

JANE AUSTEN IN MANHATTAN

Anne Baxter washes Sean Young's hair

Anne Baxter, Robert Powell, Michael Wager, Sean Young, Kurt Johnson
Locations: New York City, Albany, Cohoes (N.Y.)
Shooting: January to March 1980
Premiere: London Weekend Television, July 1980

Before *The Europeans* found its long-awaited finance, the seeds of another MIP film, *Jane Austen in Manhattan*, had been sown – and this, too, followed from the success of *Hullabaloo*. At a party at the Garrick Club in London for *Hullabaloo*, Melvyn Bragg mentioned that LWT had recently acquired the rights to an unpublished juvenile play by Jane Austen. It was based on Samuel Richardson's picaresque novel *Sir Charles Grandison*.

'The actual story of the manuscript,' Ivory said, 'is not unlike the script for *Jane Austen* which Ruth subsequently wrote around it.' David Astor, the owner of the *Observer* newspaper, bought the manuscript of the play at auction in London; and LWT, having heard that it was to be sold, promptly sent someone round to Sotheby's to catch the successful bidder and put in a production offer. 'I don't know whether David Astor read or even saw the original manuscript before he bid on it,' Ivory said. 'Perhaps he did know it wasn't a complete play, just this childish thing. Certainly Melvyn Bragg couldn't have known it – otherwise why would he have sent someone to Sotheby's to put an option down on this hot property? One can imagine the lucky buyer, David Astor, turning over this little brown thing, held together with dressmakers' pins, and thinking, "What the hell!" When he feels someone plucking at his sleeve … and his feelings of relief when he hears – it must have seemed quite incredible – that LWT wanted to buy the rights for television. One can in turn imagine Melvyn Bragg getting *his* first glance – perhaps it was the same badly typed, dim Xerox copy of the MS I was given – and wondering how he could explain his enthusiasm for the ten-year-old Jane Austen's charade, obviously written for a rainy day, to his Board of Directors. And then it was time to go to the Garrick club – can you think of anywhere more appropriate? – to meet Merchant, Ivory and Jhabvala, whereupon he said to us, "You know, we've just bought the rights to this long-lost Jane Austen play – her *only* play…" And we – of course – said "How wonderful, we'll do it." They sent it to us, this hopeless mess. At which point I was all for saying, "I'm sorry, but I didn't know it was incomplete…" Meanwhile, however, Melvyn Bragg had made an announcement to the press that we were going to make it for LWT. His Board of Directors had approved the project, wheels were in motion. We couldn't easily extricate ourselves. Then we decided to forget about it for a while, hoping that it might go away. *The Europeans* intervened.'

Ruth Jhabvala, however, saw from the start the possibilities of using the fragment, rather in the way that George Trow had used the material for *Savages*, as a means of experimenting with ideas and techniques for herself, as a novelist. A proposal was prepared after the shooting of *The Europeans* and presented to LWT in New York. The story was to be set among various quarters of the New York theatre community, rival groups were to vie for the Jane Austen manuscript, artfulness was to prevail. 'They were flabbergasted at first,' Ruth Jhabvala said, 'but then they took it very sportingly.' In the winter of 1978-79, Ruth Jhabvala worked on the script in India, separated from her partners. 'It was very complicated, I had lots of bits and pieces which I dabbled backwards, again and again. I had flashbacks within flashbacks. It was my period of greatest flashbacks: that was my favourite method. So much so that Ismail now says not a single flashback will he ever have in any film. I remember juggling scenes just for the pleasure of it really. Was the film tricky to make? Well, no one seemed to know what was what. But I did.' Like *The Europeans*, *Jane Austen* was an MIP venture in association with Polytel; its budget was $450,000, again partly underwritten by LWT. 'With that script,' Ivory said, 'I never knew where I was, in the sense that I had to pore over the script to keep track of what followed what. Ruth didn't really explain it to me. She never does. If I get it, I get it; if I don't, I don't.' In the event, Ivory did get it, although the finished film, which was generally coolly received by the British critics, was too densely literate for television's audience.

After the accomplished but cautious beginnings of *Roseland*, *Jane Austen in*

'Jane Austen in Manhattan':
Sean Young, Robert Powell

Manhattan reveals Ruth Jhabvala more confidently at home in the New York milieu. And in the way that C.S.H. Jhabvala had corrected some of the detailing of his wife's early Indian novels, so now Ivory made various amendments. 'I told her, for instance, that if, as in the script, you had young middle-class Americans living and working in the theatre, housed in a comfortable loft, these are not the kind of people in New York City today who are going to give up that loft and go jumping in the back of a truck to ride away into the sunset in the middle of winter – as she originally had them doing.' The kaleidoscopic changes between the elements of the story – the Jane Austen play has found its way into the hands of a wealthy Manhattan grant committee which has to decide which of two rival groups, each able to exercise subtle pressures on the committee, will finally produce it – are unlike any of the earlier time and place shifts, the more straightforward flashbacks, of previous MIP films.

Despite Ivory's assertion that the *Jane Austen* script is chiefly Ruth Jhabvala's, it is intriguing to note how the concerns of the MIP partnership have fused in this film. Ivory's pleasures are Ruth Jhabvala's. The company's delight in recording the process of play- and film-making is here more variegated than in *Shakespeare Wallah*, *Bombay Talkie* or *The Wild Party*; from the avant-garde, through the classical and operatic, to the Broadway musical. There is a backstage party for a Broadway first night at which, half in nervous mockery, the verdict of the *New York Times*' theatre critic is read out: shades of the insecure carryings-on at Jolly Grimm's party. And *Jane Austen* squares up to the question of the meaning of 'success' in the performing arts, just as *Hullabaloo* obliquely squared up to the meaning of the 'value' of works of fine art. Gurus reappear in various guises: though the sinister prevails, in the form of Robert Powell's seemingly satanic but intriguingly ambiguous avant-garde director, thus confirming Ruth Jhabvala's feeling, the roots of which were described in her Neil Gunn lecture, that she was coming to share Ivory's mistrustful attitude towards holy men. There is, too, a marvellous and very

**'Jane Austen in Manhattan':
the grant committee**

New York dinner party (again set in a loft*), at which the conversation among the urbane members of the committee and Lilianna, the grande dame classical director (Anne Baxter, with relish), is peppered with *trouvailles* similar to those of the Savages' climactic dinner. A chic black lady, elegantly trousered, hovers in attendance – as knowing and in control of her master George, the susceptible chairman of the grant committee, as ever the Forest Girl turned maid was, in her different way, in control of her corner of affairs at the Great House in *Savages*.

Jane Austen, which is distinguished like almost all MIP's films by the freshness of its youthful players, is a sly celebration of double-dealing. This is, however, much more complicated and intangible than that laid out in *Hullabaloo* or *The Europeans*. People – and notably the limping avant-garde director – are not just playing games on one another, working through their ambitions, but are sometimes, genuinely, not what they appear. As in a picaresque novel, trapdoors are forever opening and characters, manipulated by the unseen author, tipped unceremoniously into unexpected scenes. Loyalties (the rival directors are involved in poaching each other's players) are tested and found wanting, but also tested and sometimes found unexpectedly true; characters are manipulated – the maternal Lilianna delights in cajoling George, the affected but overwhelmingly charming mother's boy, and he delights in being cajoled – all with the peculiar ease and vigour of a genuine 18th-century novel.

In all the rumpus, that unproducable fragment of a Jane Austen play is skilfully made to do service as a hint – produced as a Mozartian opera and an avant-garde piece set in a padded cell – of something much more substantial. Another sleight of hand.

JI: All the important sets are lofts: the poor young actors live in a warehouse under the Brooklyn Bridge; George Midash, the millionaire angel, in a fabulous horizontal 'town house' crammed with objets d'art on the top floor of another commercial building on lower Fifth Avenue; Lilianna lives a few blocks south in the Village in her own loft, where she conducts acting classes for a chosen few and cooks her Slavonic delicacies; the avant-garde director Pierre's workshop-theatre is a loft-space off the Bowery, and so is the Sufi centre into which Ariadne drifts. I wanted to call the film *Loft Madness*, but no one would hear of it.

p.c–MIP. In association with Polytel International. *p*–IM. *d*–JI. *assoc. p*–Connie Kaiserman. *p. co-ordinator*–Wendy Glickstein. *p. manager*–Ronald Palazzo. *location manager*–Susie Simons. *workshop sequence sup*–Andrei Serban. *asst. d*–Ronald Palazzo, Janet Fishman. *sc*–RPJ; Libretto of *Sir Charles Grandison* by Jane Austen, Samuel Richardson. *ph*–Ernest Vincze; (opera sequence) Larry Pizer. *col*–Movielab. *camera op*–Don Sweeney. *ed*–David E. McKenna. *a.d*–Jeremiah Rusconi. *stage settings*–Michael Yeargan. *m*–Richard Robbins. *songs*–'It's Alright', 'Stay Beside Me' by and performed on the guitar by Katrina Hodiak; 'Here We Are Again' by Carmine Stippo, performed by Kurt Johnson. *singers*–(soprano) Jane Bryden, (mezzo) Joyce Andrews, (tenor) Frank Hoffmeister, (bass) David Evitts. *cost*–Jenny Beavan. *choreo*–Michael Shawn. *make-up*–Jeanne Richmond. *title design*–Hillsberg & Meyer. *sd*–Cabell Smith; (music) Media Sound. *sd. re-rec*–Jack Higgins. *Jack-of-all-trades*–Mark Potter Jr. *p. assistant*–Walter Hunnewell, Roger Barrera, Rajeev Talwani. *l.p*–Anne Baxter (*Lilianna Zorska*), Robert Powell (*Pierre*), Michael Wager (*George Midash*), Tim Choate (*Jamie*), John Guerrasio (*Gregory*), Katrina Hodiak (*Katya*), Kurt Johnson (*Victor*), Philip Lenkowsky (*Fritz*), Charles McCaughan (*Billy*), Nancy New (*Jenny*), Sean Young (*Ariadne*), Bernard Barrow (*Polson*), Lee Doyle (*Jarvis*), Bella Jarrett (*Klein*), Naomi Riordan (*Mrs Polson*), David Redden (*Auctioneer*), Gael Hammer and Peter McPherson (*Unsuccessful Bidders*), John Boyle and Tim Burke (*Chair Carriers*), Iman (*Sufi Leader*), Brenda Holmes, Michon Peacock and Christina Stolberg (*Dancers*), Michael Shawn (*Choreographer*), Susan Hovey (*Marianne*), Sarallen (*Fairbanks*), Jacquelyn Roberts (*Miss Auberry*), Sandra Seacat (*Thrift-shop Lady*), James Raitt (*Pianist*), Wayne Tuthill (*Clergyman's Clerk*). 111 mins. (35mm).

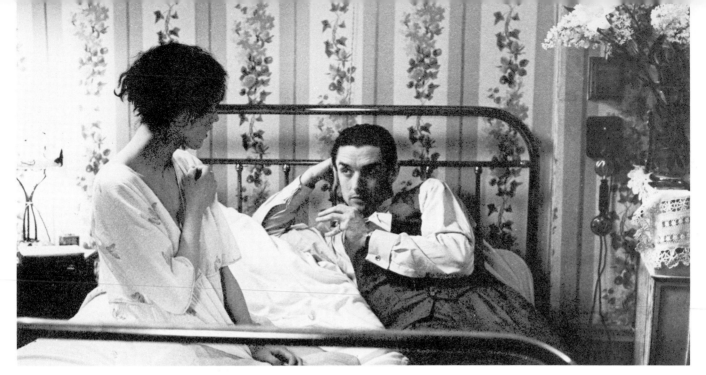

QUARTET

Isabelle Adjani, Alan Bates, Maggie Smith, Anthony Higgins
Locations: Paris and environs
Shooting: October to December 1980
Premiere: Cannes Film Festival, May 1981

One criticism made of MIP's next film, *Quartet*, an adaptation by Ruth Jhabvala of the semi-autobiographical novel by Jean Rhys detailing the unhappy course of her relationship with Ford Madox Ford, was that its heroine, Marya Zelli, was not true to the original, that she had been softened. 'This might be a valid criticism,' Ivory said, 'if there had been only one book in which Jean Rhys had written about herself. But if you think of all those women in all those novels. They are all resilient; they go from stage to stage, each stage worse than the one before, but they do get through. They are there. The intelligent suffering woman who is able to talk about what has happened to her. I don't think the change we wrought on Marya had to do with Ruth softening the character – although, while admiring Jean Rhys as a writer, she did find her low-spirited and she did think *Quartet*'s subject matter depressing. It was the casting of Isabelle Adjani as Marya that changed the part. If you had had an English intelligence there, that particular Jean Rhys intelligence, then no matter how Ruth had adapted the novel I think you would have felt it

'Quartet': Alan Bates

was closer to the Jean Rhys original. Ruth didn't change the overall story a great deal, but the soul of the narrator, as played by a Latin woman, did change.'

At the start of *Jane Austen* in Sotheby Parke Bernet, after the successful bid for the manuscript, one hears the announcement of the next lot, a parcel of letters between Jean Rhys and Ford Madox Ford. The notion of making *Quartet* had been in the air for three or four years; the rights were obtained without difficulty and had, Ivory said, provided Jean Rhys with one of her last pieces of income before her death. Ruth Jhabvala began work on the script soon after *The Europeans* (it is now a Merchant Ivory habit, such is still the uncertainty of finance, to have at least one script in preparation while another is being filmed). Ivory was the project's motive force. He had been introduced to Jean Rhys's novels by Ruth Jhabvala, and like her with *Jane Austen* he saw something in *Quartet* for himself. Paris the great cosmopolitan artistic centre of the 1920s, the Paris of Hemingway's *A Moveable Feast*. And in keeping with the backbiting as well as elegiac tone of Hemingway's memoir, a Hemingway figure, unflatteringly sketched, crops up in Rhys's novel and Ivory's film. It is not a civilisation in decay, or even one at a particularly decadent period (although several smooth and unsavoury characters glide through the film, the sort of brilliantined shysters seen on the fringes of Jolly Grimm's wild party). It is in fact a sort of Golden Age, but this time a dramatic one.*

Rather as Ruth Jhabvala felt a relief at being able in *Roseland* to write dialogue for characters who spoke English to other people who spoke English, one feels in *Quartet* that Ivory had in a way at last come home. The Heidlers (Alan Bates and Maggie Smith), he a writer-critic, she an artist, who befriend the waiflike Marya when her husband is jailed for trafficking in antiques, are people for whom Ivory seems to have an instinctive understanding. Although settled in Paris, they are at heart nomads, the sort of people most at home in restaurants, nightclubs and cafés. Matters are brought to a head between the cloakroom and the bar; women confide (as they did in *Roseland*) in the powder room; Marya auditions for a part she will never get in the office of two polite but indifferent impresarios (the world of entertainment is as impermanent as the world of the expatriate artists inhabiting a seductive Paris of *hôtels particuliers*). Ivory relishes this Paris – a Paris of the imagination, lacking the gritty unpleasantness of Jean Rhys's Paris – and he relishes its decor.

Quartet also treated that enduring Merchant Ivory theme, patronage, and in a less tangible sense the propensity of people to take up others. Lucia Lane in *Bombay Talkie* took up the film star Vikram, and briefly the writer Hari, there was any amount of 'taking up' in *Jane Austen*, Clark Haven set himself to woo the Maharani in *Hullabaloo*, Julian Branch in *Savages* had been taken up by the Hostess. Here the Heidlers take up Marya: he because of a fatal susceptibility to young women; his wife, realising this, as a means of holding on to him. The

JI: It was this Golden Age aspect of Paris between the wars that attracted me to *Quartet* and, for that matter, to Jean Rhys. It has always interested me. When I first arrived in Paris in 1950 you could still sense that Golden Age, despite the 1939-45 war. Many people were around who had figured prominently in it, weren't even very old yet. You could touch it, smell it, and Paris hadn't yet been modernised. It was exciting. Most Americans of my generation who went there then felt that (kids no longer do). That is why *An American in Paris* was such a big delight and a big hit back home. People were crazy about Paris, wanted to go there just as I did, in the same way that they wanted to go to Rome a few years later, and to London in the 1960s. And I arrived in Paris straight from Oregon. I had never been in a big city like that. San Francisco didn't count. I don't think it was nostalgia for a bygone time that we felt, because it wasn't bygone. Twenties Paris is supposed to have finished with the 1929 stock market crash, and no doubt Thirties Paris ended with the Occupation, but we didn't care. Having said that, however, it is the *story* of *Quartet* which made the film worth doing, not the attractions of reconstructing Paris in 1927. That is where I found something for myself: in those lives.

'Quartet': Maggie Smith (right)

cruelty with which Heidler pigeonholes Marya is the obverse of the true friendship which Merchant Ivory characters, so often trapped by social or cultural conventions, have sought. The sense is of people trying to belong in worlds which are not wholly their own. Marya is in a way the classic MIP heroine, floating between a number of worlds which are not her own, floating and surviving, as Jean Rhys had done.

Ivory: 'I sat at our "wrap" party the last night of shooting in Paris – it was very late, already 2 a.m., and the crew members were one by one making ringing orations about Art and Friendship in deep French voices – and I thought about Jean Rhys and also about all of us. There we were, more than fifty years after the sad events described in *Quartet* had taken place, this big roomful of English and French film technicians, actors, financiers, all full of good food and drink, full of the film we had made, sure that everything we were doing was absolutely the right thing to be doing, secure – as far as I knew – in our jobs, homes, love relationships. I wondered what we all had to do with Jean Rhys, who seemed never to have had any of these things.

'A long time ago she had desperately loved an important man, he had coldly

JI: Yes, I relished the 'flavour', as well as the decor and was criticised for my enthusiasm. Perhaps the critics preferred to watch the decor and fashions so they could escape the story, which was unedifying. Anyway, if you're going to make a period film, you *have* to try and get everything right if you can. It's never more than an approximation in any case, for the purpose of creating atmosphere. You do it for its own sake sometimes because it's one of the ingredients of the 'entertainment value' and a powerful one when done well. Otherwise, 'getting it right' can be a very frustrating exercise and a damned nuisance. The big thing that we could never get right on *Quartet* on our budget were Paris streets. It seemed to me as if the ground floor of every building in Paris except Notre Dame had recently had a face-lift, that every lobby door in every seedy hotel of my youth has been changed to plate glass, and as for the sidewalk cafés, apart from Les Deux Magots where we couldn't work, they're all gone, just like that – the 'sidewalk' part, anyway. 'Protected' by plate-glass walls – a recent French mania – and disfigured by ugly hanging lamps with orange plastic shades and rocking to high-decibel video games, but bearing resonant names like The Dome, The Select, and the Café Flore, these establishments seem to be waiting for some future Minister of Culture to rescue them from their present unhappy status.

thrown her over, her jail-bird husband had broken with her, and, to ease the pain, she said, she wrote about it and in due course it became *Quartet*. Then she moved on – to other men, another country, to other books; grew old, dropped from sight, was forgotten, was rediscovered, then honoured briefly, and died – by all accounts poor. I could not help thinking that just the scenes we would in all likelihood cut out were probably, in terms of cost, more than her lifetime earnings had been, even allowing for a half century of inflation. Something was wrong somewhere. Yet I feel that if Jean Rhys had lived she would have approved of the film. She would not have minded the distancing from herself that Isabelle Adjani brought to the part of Marya Zelli, and on the other hand she would have approved of Adjani's beauty, and of her nature that comes across on the screen with such intensity in this and other films.'

Ivory's *Quartet* cost $1.8m, the money coming from Gaumont in Paris, 20th Century-Fox in London and Roger Corman's New World Pictures in Los Angeles. Photographed by Pierre Lhomme, it is marked by a graceful fluidity. The manner, for instance, in which the camera weaves through the nightclub at which the blues singer Armelia McQueen is entertaining (and Ivory, having found a favourite moment, lets the scene run) bears no comparison to the nightclub scene in *Bombay Talkie*, in which another singer is allowed to get to the end of her number. The *Bombay Talkie* scene has other interests, but that in *Quartet* is savoured for itself – just as, one imagines, the Heidlers and their rich fellow expatriates relished the 'flavour' of the Paris of the 1920s.*

p.c–MIP/Lyric International (Paris). *p*–IM, Jean-Pierre Mahot de la Querantonnais. *d*–JI. *exec. p*–Hubert Niogret. *assoc. p*–Humbert Balsan, Connie Kaiserman. *p. controller*–Alain Depardieu. *location scout*–Jacques Quinternet. *asst. d*–Hughes de Laugardière. *sc*–RPJ. Based on the novel by Jean Rhys. *French dial*–Michel Maingois. *ph*–Pierre Lhomme. *col*–GTC. *camera op*–Philippe Brun. *ed*–Humphrey Dixon. *a.d*–Jean-Jacques Caziot. *set dresser*–Robert Christides. *portraits*–Jean de Gramont, François Marcepoil. *picture assistant*–Angélique Armand-Delille. *m*–Richard Robbins; 'Arabesque valsante' by Mischa Levitsky. *songs*–'The 509', 'Full-time Lover' arranged by Luther Henderson, performed by Armelia McQueen; 'Pars' by Jean Lenoir, performed by Isabelle Adjani; 'L'Air des bijoux' by Boris Gounod, performed by Sophie de Segur. *m.d/m. arrangements*–Vic Flick. *choreo*–Elisabeth Aldridge. *cost*–Judy Moorcroft. *make-up*–Kenneth Lintott, Tommy Manderson. *sd. ed*–David Renton. *sd. rec*–Bernard Bats. *m. rec*–John Richards. *sd. re-rec*–Richard King. *sd. assistant*–Alan Coddington. *English subtitles*–Titra-Film. *l.p*–Isabelle Adjani (*Marya Zelli*), Anthony Higgins (*Stephan Zelli*), Maggie Smith (*Lois Heidler*), Alan Bates (*H. J. Heidler*), Pierre Clémenti (*Théo the Pornographer*), Daniel Mesguich (*Pierre Schlamovitz*), Virginie Thevenet (*Mlle Chardin*), Suzanne Flon (*Mme Hautchamp*), Sebastien Floche (*M Hautchamp*), Sheila Gish (*Anna*), Daniel Chatto (*Guy*), Paulita Sedgwick (*Esther*), Bernice Stegers (*Miss Nicholson*), Isabelle Canto Da Maya ('*Cri-Cri*'), François Viaur (*Lefranc*), Wiley Wood (*Cairn*), Dino Zanghi, Michel Such and Jean-Pierre Dravel (*Prison Guards*), Annie Noël (*Maid*), Maurice Ribot (*Pianist*), Pierre Julien (*Impresario*), Humbert Balsan (*Impresario's Friend*), Serge Marquand (*Nightclub Owner*), Armelia McQueen (*Nightclub Singer*), Muriel Montosse (*Marjorie*), Caroline Loeb ('*Nun*'), Jeffrey Kime (*James*), Shirley Allan (*Adriana*), Anne-Marie Brissonière, Marie-France de Bourges and Brigitte Hermetz (*Les Oiseaux*), Joceline Comellas (*Café Patronne*), Romain Bremond (*Youth*), Arlette Spetelbroot (*Drowned Girl*), Monique Mauclair (*Hotel Concierge*). 101 mins. (35mm). English and French dialogue/English subtitles.

HEAT AND DUST

The Nawab's banquet

Julie Christie, Shashi Kapoor, Greta Scacchi, Christopher Cazenove
Locations: Hyderabad; Gulmarg (Kashmir); London
Shooting: February to April, August 1982
Premiere: London, January 1983

'I feel,' Ivory said, 'that *The Europeans* is Ruth's, *Quartet* is mine and *Heat and Dust* is Ismail's.' Merchant's partners dragged their feet – it seemed, Ivory said, as if MIP was going over old ground in *Heat and Dust* – and had to be spurred on by the producer who had secured various deals with the Rank Organisation, the Curzon cinema in London (which had done record business with *The Europeans*) and several other sources, some in India. Merchant wanted, was determined, to make an Indian film to mark Merchant Ivory's twenty-first year of production.

Heat and Dust intertwines many threads from MIP's earlier films. The book was up to a point written out of the partnership of Merchant, Ivory and Ruth Jhabvala. In *The Householder*, Ernest, the bright-eyed, loose-limbed young American who had come to India to submerge himself in the mystic wonder of it all, is left with his dreams intact. He visits a roadside guru who looks upon him benevolently, not altogether seriously. In *Heat and Dust*, that same young American reappears, only now he is genuinely infected by India: he has gone the whole way, changed his name to Chidananda, shaved his head and

'Heat and Dust': Charles
McCaughan

'Heat and Dust': Christopher Cazenove

adopted saffron robes. But unlike Ernest, who lived in a safe Western household, Chid personifies a contradiction: he claims not to need money, but of course he must have it and has no conscience about taking it; he has cleansed his body, but he is still troubled by lust – like many of Ruth Jhabvala's holy men he has an intense comical sexual drive. In the end, he succumbs to India. He becomes really ill, is forced to consult an Indian doctor (who attends to him with the weary knowingness of the British doctor who treated the benighted Indians in the 1920s story), and then throws in the sponge – is last seen on a departing train, defeated, babbling about the comforts of family life in the Midwest, returning to security.

In *The Householder*, Prem faced up to the duties of family life. In *Heat and Dust*, for reasons, Indian reasons, not entirely clear, the Nawab of Khatm* has been separated from his wife ('She was too young for me' – a comment Prem might have made) and, having no family duties, spends his time, in true MIP fashion, intriguing. In *Shakespeare Wallah*, a rich young Indian, Sanju, dallies with a susceptible English girl: her parents, old India hands, intervene and send her packing to England. In *Heat and Dust*, the Nawab – which role, together with those of Prem and Sanju, is taken by Shashi Kapoor – sets himself to woo a young married Englishwoman, older than Lizzie in *Shakespeare Wallah* but if anything less sophisticated, and seduces her. Her parents – in the shape of the experienced British male administrators of the Raj and their faithful spouses – find out too late what has happened and are unable to send her packing since she has left the Civil Lines of her own accord. But they do the next best thing which is to pretend she never existed. The charm of Sanju and the Nawab, a paradoxical charm, stems from the fact that they are both disarmingly polite (generously polite in a wholly unBritish way) but at the same time idle, watchful, imperceptibly dangerous. The Nawab chides his guest Harry for not paying his card debts with a genuine childlike affection; but later, when Harry seems to him to be behaving like a spoilt child who has gone off in a huff, when he returns to his own people in preparation for leaving India, the Nawab is equally capable of ordering him back to the palace as if he was a child in such a way that he cannot be gainsaid. It is the fascination of this charm – and Shashi Kapoor, with his turban and his spotted bowtie, his beguiling English Indianness, is in sympathy with the part – which holds the film-makers.

Heat and Dust reverberates, too, with fainter echoes. Anne, the capable woman of the modern story, is discovered before a narrow mirror being instructed how to wear a sari. Olivia, Anne's susceptible great-aunt, visiting the Nawab's palace and the sick Harry, glances at the paintings on the wall of the bedroom – 'Come away, come away,' Harry says, they are erotic paintings, a bride being prepared for her husband. ('This is my most precious and private collection…') Indu in *The Householder* almost disgraced her husband with the cakes at the tea party; Olivia, at her first durbar, takes more than a ritual pinch

JI: The Hindustani names in our films are straightforward almost to the point of simple-mindedness: *Khatm* means 'finished', 'all over'. Satipur, the other town in *Heat and Dust*, would be the place known for one or more *suttees*; the *Tasveer* collection in *Hullabaloo* means, literally, the picture collection, etc.

of the traditional refreshments and almost disgraces her husband Douglas, until she is saved by the Burrah Memsahib's discreetly proferred handkerchief. There is a correspondence, too, between Douglas and Prem, Indu's husband: both are newly married, relatively lowly civil servants, possessed of dreamy wives, beset by conventions they cannot transcend. In *Heat and Dust*, a palace dinner party, peppered with overheard anecdotes, climaxes with the stamping entry of a band of Indian bagpipers, Scottish Indians, playing the jaunty anthem of Khatm. Their presence is a natural incongruity, as natural as Georgie dressing up as Father Christmas.

Ruth Jhabvala's reconciliation with India is encapsulated in a scene in the novel of *Heat and Dust* in which an old beggarwoman dies. (A version of this scene was shot for the film but later dropped.) She dies in squalor but she dies with a certain appropriateness: her time has come. The beggarwoman dies; Anne, who has become pregnant by the married man, Inder Lal, in whose house she has lodged during her researches, decides against abortion and to have her baby in India, in the mountains of Kashmir where her great-aunt lived out her days without the comfort of the Nawab's unborn children. The film ends on a note of optimism. The future has been embraced. But the central mystery of *Heat and Dust* is how Olivia, having left Douglas and having ensconced herself in Kashmir, cut off from the West, with only, it seems, her piano and occasional visits from her Nawab for company, occupied her mind. Why was she so apparently happy? Perhaps like the beggarwoman she accepted her imperfect fate. It is characteristic of Merchant Ivory Productions that we are left to make up our own minds.

---

p.c–MIP. *p*–IM. *d*–JI. *assoc. p*–Rita Mangat, Connie Kaiserman. *asst. to p*–Paul Bradley. *p. co-ordinator*–Shama Habibullah. *p. manager*–Peter Manley. *location manager*–Deepak Nayar. *asst. d*–Kevan Baker; David Nichols, Gopal Ram. *sc*–RPJ. Based on her own novel. *Urdu dialogue*–Saeed Jaffrey. *Hindi dialogue*–Harish Khare. *continuity*–Jane Buck. *ph*–Walter Lassally. In colour. *camera asst*–Tony Garrett, Rajesh Joshi. *ed*–Humphrey Dixon; (asst) Mark Potter Jr. *p. designer*–Wilfred Shingleton. *a.d*–Maurice Fowler, Ram Yadekar. *set dresser*–Agnes Fernandes. *props*–Tom Freeman. *stills*–Christopher Cormack. *m/m.d*–Richard Robbins. *assoc. m.d*–Zakir Hussain. *musicians*–Pandit Chaurasia (flute), Sultan Khan (sarangi), Nishat Khan (sitar), Zakir Hussain (percussion), Michael Reeves (piano), Mick Parker (synthesizer), Ameer Mohammed Khan (singer), Harry Rabinowitz (conductor). *cost*–Barbara Lane; (asst) Mary Ellis. *make-up*–Gordon Kay; (asst) Mohamed Amir. *hairdresser*–Carol Hemming; (asst) Jeffrey Haines.

titles–Camera Effects. *title art*–Eyre & Hobhouse. *sd. ed*–Brian Blamey, (asst) Tony Bray. *sd. rec*–Ray Beckett. *sd. re-rec*–Richard King. *asst. to d*–Prashant Gupta. *p. assistants*–Nancy Vanden Berg, Piyush Patel. *cast*–(The 1920s: In the Civil Lines at Satipur) Christopher Cazenove (*Douglas Rivers*), Greta Scacchi (*Olivia*), Julian Glover (*Mr Crawford*), Susan Fleetwood (*Mrs Crawford*), Patrick Godfrey (*Dr Saunders*), Jennifer Kendal (*Mrs Saunders*); (At the Palace in Khatm) Shashi Kapoor (*The Nawab*), Madhur Jaffrey (*The Begum*), Nickolas Grace (*Harry*), Barry Foster (*Major Minnies*), Amanda Walker (*Lady Mackleworth*), Sudha Chopra (*Chief Princess*), Sajid Khan (*Dacoit Chief*), Daniel Chatto (*Guy*); (The 1980s: In Satipur town) Julie Christie (*Anne*), Zakir Hussain (*Inder Lal*), Ratna Pathak (*Rita, Inder Lal's wife*), Tarla Mehta (*Inder Lal's Mother*), Charles McCaughan (*Chidananda*), Parveen Paul (*Maji*), Jayant Kripilani (*Dr Gopal*), Leelabhai (*Leelavati*). 130 mins. (35mm).

'Heat and Dust': (top) Shashi Kapoor and guests; (middle) Greta Scacchi; (bottom) Julie Christie and Zakir Hussain

In Pavan Pool

THE COURTESANS OF BOMBAY

Saeed Jaffrey, Zohra Segal
Location: Bombay, Safipur (U.P.)
Shooting: January, February, December 1981, January to April, Sept. 1982
Premiere: London, January 1983

**'The Courtesans of Bombay':
Ismail Merchant directs**

The 80-year-old singer of Jaisalmer, whom we hear at the end of *Autobiography of a Princess*, and whose unquenchably cheerful face we take away with us as the film's last image, may have lost her youth and her looks, but she still has her art. The courtesans of Pavan Pool in Bombay, one of the last sprawling enclosed communities of singers and musicians and their families remaining in India, have fallen on hard times, and now, it seems, their pride in their art will not sustain them for much longer. When he was a boy Ismail Merchant had heard the courtesans outside the community in which they now chiefly entertain. He had become enraptured, and some forty years later decided, without a clear plan in mind, to make a film about them. The landlord of Pavan Pool, Kareem Samar, a friend, approved the project, and in 1980 Merchant began to direct sequences of the daily life of the community and the performances of its members. 'One interest of this film,' Ivory said, 'is that it records a unique form of Indian entertainment, Indian art, which has come down until recently virtually unchanged. You can see some girls of Pavan Pool dancing exactly as the courtesans danced in the Indian miniature paintings.'

The Courtesans of Bombay, which was completed with finance from Channel 4 in London, knits up several MIP themes. The bribable rent-collector, a Ruth Jhabvala favourite, and here a not unlikable character as played by Kareem Samar, cropped up in *The Householder*; the dissolute connoisseur (Saeed Jaffrey) – a second-rate actor, it is suggested, 'whose face you may have seen in the Urdu cinema…' – has assumed numerous guises. The question, What constitutes artistic success, achievement? has been asked before. The coming girls of Pavan Pool are neglecting their mothers' arts, the old disciplines, in favour of disco dancing. No women are admitted as members of the audience and the men, who slip away from their wives to listen to the girls and sometimes (though a veil is drawn by the film) purchase their favours, have grown less discriminating as patrons. There are, however, some performers – and two such, Uma and Shanti Bai, close the film with bravura performances – who can still command a following. The Bombay film world has taken its toll; the girls now wish to sing and dance for the movies, the community ties are slipping. But, as the Saeed Jaffrey character observes, there was only one Nimmi and there are thousands of courtesans. They wait in vain for the big producer with the contract. There is, however, in Pavan Pool a faded but still palpable vitality: despite the preponderance of loafing young men (the birth of a baby girl is celebrated, a future bread-winner; that of a boy, a mouth to feed, is not), the entertainers show a spirit not unlike that of some of the dispossessed Maharajas and Maharanis of *Autobiography of a Princess*.*

The Courtesans of Bombay is rough hewn. And it has something of the flavour and immediacy of a story in today's newspaper. The fictional characters are there chiefly as a means of telegraphing information (though one of them, Zohra Segal, who played the holy woman to Madhur Jaffrey's slighted wife in *The Guru*, gives a winning performance, full of coquettish good humour, as the retired courtesan who talks about her life while at the same time lecturing us about the correct preparation of lime pickle). From time to time, however, the film is flecked with moments which suggest a mystery. Despite all their privations, and the intimations of the community's dissolution, the entertainers, the true entertainers, will probably survive. Everything pales to insignificance, time stops, when the singer Shanti Bai, no longer in her first youth, performs and her listeners sigh and flick their wrists in ecstasy. The performer meets her moment.

---

p.c–MIP. For Channel 4. *p/d*–IM. *assoc. p*–Kareem Samar, Wahid Chowhan. *asst. d*–Michael Fields. *devised by*–IM, JI, RPJ. *ph*–Vishnu Mathur. In colour. *2nd Unit cameraman*–Rajesh Joshi. *asst. cameraman*–Gyanchand Rikki. *ed*–Amit Bose. *asst. ed*–Anna Ksiezopolska, Julie Talen, Sunil Roy. *titles*–Camera Effects. *sd. rec*–Ray Beckett. *sd. re-rec*–Richard King. *asst. to d*–Aamer Hussein. *with*–Saeed Jaffrey, Zohra Segal, Kareem Samar, the people of Pavan Pool, Bombay. 73 mins. (16mm).

JI: *The Courtesans of Bombay* and *Autobiography of a Princess* are similar in that they started out as straightforward documentaries and then veered into the area of fiction film through incorporating staged scenes with actors. Originally, in *Autobiography* the James Mason-Madhur Jaffrey dialogue was planned to frame the Royal India archive footage, to show it off and put it in context. But the frame became the picture. With *The Courtesans*, however, the real-life footage holds centre stage, with the actors only coming forward occasionally to comment on the residents of Pavan Pool, and on the community's society and traditions. In subject matter, *The Courtesans* also somewhat resembles *Roseland*, in that it takes the audience into a strange, half-lit, predominantly lower-middle-class world most people don't know much about – or if they do, it's with feelings of disdain – a world that only comes alive at night, moves to a musical beat, and operates within an elaborate etiquette of its own, and within a system of compromises – economic and emotional – few of us are called upon to make.

The Courtesans of Bombay

ACKNOWLEDGMENTS

For help in the preparation of this book, the author's thanks are due to: Contemporary Films, Enterprise Pictures, the Stills Department of the National Film Archive, Merchant Ivory Productions, Rachel Marks, Tristram Powell, Chloe Taylor, Carol Taylor, Hope Pym, David Wilson, Geoffrey Nowell-Smith, Mary Lea Bandy, Ruth Prawer Jhabvala, Ismail Merchant, James Ivory and Edwin Taylor. Picture credits: Frank Herrmann, Fred Ohringer (MIP), Sylvia Norris (Ismail Merchant and Agnes Moorehead), Suresh Sheth (*Bombay Talkie*), BBC TV (*Adventures of a Brown Man in Search of Civilisation*), Mary Ellen Mark (*Hullabaloo Over Georgie and Bonnie's Pictures*), Christopher Cormack (*Heat and Dust*), Karan Kapoor (*The Courtesans of Bombay*). Pictures in Chapter One courtesy of Paramount Pictures, MGM, 20th Century-Fox, Columbia, Universal and Warner Bros.